Introduction

Links with the programme of study for Citizenship at Key Stage 4

This chart shows which books in the *Citizenship in Focus* series cover particular areas of knowledge and understanding required in the programmes of study at Key Stage 4 to enable students to become informed citizens.

Requirement	Coverage	Example
The legal and human rights and responsibilities that underpin society	*The Citizen and the Law*; *Human Rights*	What are human rights?, page 1, *Human Rights*
The need for mutual understanding and respect in a multicultural society	*Human Rights*; *The Citizen and the Law*	Race discrimination, page 25, *Human Rights*
The work of parliament, the government and the courts in making and shaping the law	*Democracy in Action*; *The Citizen and the Law*	How a law is made, page 5, *Democracy in Action*
The importance of playing an active part in democratic and electoral processes	*Democracy in Action*	A democratic deficit?, page 14, *Democracy in Action*
How the economy works – government finances, the international financial system	*Democracy in Action*; *Global Concerns*	Currencies and exchange rates, page 10, *Global Concerns*
The opportunities for individuals and voluntary groups to bring about social change	*Global Concerns*; *Human Rights*; *Democracy in Action*	Pressure groups, page 20, *Democracy in Action*
The importance of a free press and the role of the media in providing information and influencing opinion	*Global Concerns*; *Human Rights*; *Democracy in Action*	Both sides of the story?, page 21, *Global Concerns*
The rights and responsibilities of consumers, employers and employees	*The Citizen and the Law*	Consumers and the law, page 8, *The Citizen and the Law*
The UK's relations with the EU and other European states, with the Commonwealth and the UN	*Democracy in Action*; *Global Concerns*	The UK and the European Union, page 27, *Democracy in Action*
The issues and challenges of global interdependence and responsibility	*Global Concerns*	Interdependence – the key to our survival, page 31, *Global Concerns*

Introduction

Aims of the series

The *Citizenship in Focus* series provides the student with basic knowledge and understanding of those key aspects of society with which citizenship education is concerned. *Democracy in Action* aims to develop political literacy by discussing how democratic institutions function, and by examining the skills and values relevant to active participation in a democracy. *The Citizen and the Law* aims to provide a basic knowledge and understanding both of the British legal system and how it works, and of a person's legal rights and responsibilities in public and private life. *Human Rights* aims to develop understanding of human rights issues relating to freedom of expression and religious belief, economic rights, social rights and civil rights. *Global Concerns* aims to provide an understanding of the major problems facing the world at the start of the twenty-first century and to increase awareness of the impact of globalisation.

Citizenship at Key Stage 4

Together the books provide a detailed coverage of the requirements for citizenship education at Key Stage 4. They provide information about the legal, political, social, constitutional and economic systems that influence people's lives, examining how they work and their effects. They also offer the students opportunities to think about and to discuss topical political, moral, social and cultural issues. For example, *Democracy in Action* provides information about the work of Parliament, about different electoral systems and the proposals for constitutional change as well as about other important contemporary issues such as devolution and Britain's relationship with the European Union. In *The Citizen and the Law* the operation of the criminal and civil justice systems is explained

and the different ways that laws affect individuals as neighbours, consumers, employers and employees are explored. *Human Rights* examines the rights and responsibilities underpinning society and investigates a wide range of human rights issues, ranging from freedom of religious belief to freedom from discrimination and the right to life. *Global Concerns* provides an international perspective on social issues, introducing the concepts of global interdependence and responsibility, providing information on world problems, such as population, poverty, health and hunger.

The Teacher's Resources Book

The *Teacher's Resources* book is designed to provide teachers with ideas on how to develop the activities and information given in the three students' books. In addition to notes on the units covered in each book, the resource book also contains 48 copymasters, twelve per book, each relating to a particular unit, which can be photocopied free of charge for use within the school. The copymasters offer a variety of supplementary materials, including projects for the pupils to undertake, questionnaires to complete, newspaper articles to analyse and discuss, and suggestions for writing and role plays. They are designed to get students to explore actively the issues that have been raised in order to develop their skills, their knowledge and understanding.

> The unit notes contain suggestions for Internet and keyword searches, providing keywords marked with a **SEARCH**. These are keywords to use when searching for additional information on the Internet. Go to a site with a search engine (e.g. www.yahoo.co.uk) and type in a keyword, e.g. 'parliament' or set of keywords 'Welsh + assembly + elections'. In order to restrict the search, it may be useful to set the search engine on UK sites only at first.

Teacher's Resources

New curriculum edition

in FOCUS

Published by HarperCollins*Publishers* Ltd
77–85 Fulham Palace Road
London W6 8JB

www.**Collins**Education.com
On-line support for schools and colleges

© HarperCollins*Publishers* Ltd 2000

First published 1999

This revised and expanded edition 2000

Reprinted 2001

ISBN 0 00 327 363 6

British Library Cataloguing in Publication Data
A catalogue record for this book is available from the British Library.

Commissioned by Thomas Allain-Chapman

Project managed by Gaynor Spry

Edited by Melanie McRae

Cover design and page layout by Ken Vail Graphic Design, Cambridge

Illustrations by Phil Burrows, Steve Smith

Printed and bound by Martins the Printers, Berwick-upon-Tweed

You might also like to visit www.fireandwater.co.uk
The book lover's website

Acknowledgements

The publishers gratefully acknowledge the following for permission to reproduce copyright material. Every effort has been made to trace copyright holders, but in some cases has proved impossible. The publishers would be happy to hear from any copyright holder that has not been acknowledged.

Exctract 'Bananas: The Facts' is from an article 'We're Going Bananas' taken from the 'New Internationalist October 1999'. © New Internationalist. Reprinted by permission of The Guardian.

Extract from 'Learning Lies out of reach for 125m of World's poorest children' taken from The Guardian, 31 January 2000. © The Guardian. Reprinted with permission.

Article 'Euthanasia is a job for executioners not doctors' taken from 'Daily Telegraph 7 December 1999. © Telegraph Group Limited 1997. Reprinted with permission.

Extract 'Project Censored rated the news – again' is taken from 'Censored 1999'. Reprinted by permission of Project Censored, Sociology Dept, Sanoma State University.

Extract 'Plan to fight child porn criticised' is taken from BBC News Online. Reprinted courtesy of BBC News Online http://news.bbc.co.uk

Extract 'Legit hackers roam cyberspace for security' by Paul de Bendern.

Extracts relating to 'Cool Planet Website' reprinted by permission of Oxfam.

Extracts relating to 'Passports for Pets' reprinted by permission of Passports for Pets.

Collins

Simon **Foster**
John **Foster**

Contents

Copymasters

Democracy in Action

Democracy – the citizens decide (p. 1)

Aim: To explain what democracy means and the distinction between direct democracy and representative democracy.

Copymaster 1: Setting up a school council offers guidelines on how to set up a school council, including deciding who shall be represented and how many representatives each group should have. If the school already has a school council, students can look critically at its constitution, discuss how democratic it is and put forward suggestions as to how it could be reformed.

Britain's system of government (p. 2)

Aim: To explain that Britain is a constitutional monarchy and the difference between presidential and parliamentary government.

Copymaster 2: The monarchy – what are the facts? consists of 12 statements about the monarch, some of which are true and some are false. The answers are: 1 True. 2 False. 3 True. 4 False. 5 True. 6 False. 7 False. 8 False. 9 False. 10 False. 11 True. 12 False. Students could research the arguments for and against reform or abolition of the monarchy and debate the issue.

SEARCH Keywords: monarchy, republic

In groups, pupils could choose another country with a democratic system of government and research its constitution, comparing it with the British system.

Being a Member of Parliament (p. 3)

Aim: To explore what an MP does.

Students could produce a profile of their local MPs. Ask them to find out what role MPs play in Parliament and what local, regional and national issues they are particularly interested in. Groups could list the questions they would like to ask their MP, then invite them to answer their questions either in person or in writing.

The Parliamentary Education Unit, Room 604 Norman Shaw Building (North), London SW1A 2TT (e-mail: edunit@parliament.uk) publishes two useful guides for young people: *The Work of an MP* and *The Palace of Westminster*. It has also produced six education sheets: *Parliamentary Elections, The House of Commons, Parliament and Government, Making a Law, Debates in Parliament* and *The House of*

Lords, which can be found on the Internet by following links from Parliament's home page address http://www.parliament.uk

The House of Commons – making the laws (pp. 4–5)

Aim: To explain how Parliament makes laws.

Copymaster 3: How to hold a debate explains the rules of formal debating and offers students an opportunity to participate in a debate on a current issue.

SEARCH Keywords: Parliament, legislation, bills, acts

The general election (pp. 6–7)

Aim: To explain what happens at a general election.

Students could organize an election for a school Parliament. Small groups can work together as members of a party to draft a manifesto, outlining the changes they would make to how the school is run. They can then choose one of the group to be their candidate and prepare a television party political broadcast and/or a leaflet to explain their policies to the rest of the class. The election itself should incorporate a secret ballot and a returning officer.

The UK electoral system – time for a change? (pp. 8–9)

Aim: To provide information on alternative voting systems.

Copymaster 4: Changing the voting system consists of a questionnaire that pupils can use in order to survey public opinion to find out which voting system people favour.

Students could analyse the data on a computer, and write a report of their findings. After discussing their views, students could write a letter to a newspaper explaining why they are for or against reform of the voting system.

Information on the arguments for reform can be found on the Internet at Charter 88's home page http://www.charter88.org.uk and the Electoral Reform Society's home page http://www.electoral–reform.org.uk or obtained from: Charter 88, Exmouth House, 3-11 Pine Street, London EC1R 0JH and The Electoral Reform Society, 6 Chancel Street, Blackfriars, London SE1 0UU.

Regional government (pp. 10–11)

Aim: To explain devolution and what it means for different regions of the United Kingdom.

Copymaster 5: Devolution in the United Kingdom presents a questionnaire which students can use to research people's opinions on devolution. Students could use a spreadsheet or database to analyse the results by computer.

To highlight what the issues are locally, you could invite two local politicians with opposing views on regional government to visit the school to explain their positions and to answer students' questions. Students could write a newspaper report giving details of their arguments.

SEARCH Keywords: devolution, assembly, Scottish Parliament, mayor

The House of Lords (pp. 12–13)

Aim: To explain the new composition and functions of the House of Lords and explore proposals for its reform.

After discussing the issues and the various proposals for reform, students can imagine that they work for an advertising agency that has been commissioned to produce a full-page advertisement for a newspaper, clearly stating the reasons either in favour of or against further reform of the House of Lords. *Copymaster 6: A revised upper chamber* describes how the upper chambers of the USA and the UK are constituted (as of early 2000) and what their powers are, to act as the basis for students' own suggestions for further reform of the House of Lords.

How democratic is Britain's government? (pp. 14–15)

Aim: To explore whether a democratic deficit exists in the British system of government.

Students could contact the Home Office to find out about the latest suggestions for improving voter turnout. This has included electronic voting and polling stations in supermarkets.

To demonstrate how a referendum works, you could organise a referendum on a school issue, such as a proposal to extend the school day. Talk about different ways of wording the referendum, agree on a wording, hold the referendum, then ask the pupils to write what

they have learned about referenda from the experience.

Copymaster 7: Using the Internet explains how to participate in an e-mail or on-line discussion group. Students could use the Internet to find a discussion group on a particular subject (e.g. electoral reform) and then join in. They could then write a report on what they learned and present it to the class.

The finances of government (pp. 16–17)

Aim: To explain public spending and how it is financed through taxation.

Introduce the idea that taxation can also be used to try to influence people's behaviour, e.g. congestion charges for using private cars in inner city areas. Groups could discuss other ideas for 'green taxes' that would help the environment, then try to gauge how such proposals would be received by surveying public reaction to them.

Political parties (pp. 18–19)

Aim: To explore what different political parties represent.

Students could compare the British system of funding political parties with other countries and discuss whether there should be state funding of political parties. You could invite the constituency organisations of the main political parties to send representatives to talk to the students about what they stand for. Get the students to draft questions to put to the speakers, and to write a statement saying whether what they heard has influenced them to want to join a political party. www.simonfindthis.co.uk contains links to the web pages of all the UK political parties.

Pressure groups (pp. 20–21)

Aim: To understand how pressure groups operate.

Copymaster 8: Lobbying in action explains the techniques used by the pressure group Passports for Pets. Students could choose a pressure group and investigate the campaigning techniques it uses by studying the literature it produces and visiting its website. *Copymaster 9: Setting up a pressure group* takes students through the stages of setting up a pressure group and organising a campaign. In groups, students could design a website, draft a press release and write a letter to their local MP asking for their support.

(SEARCH) Keywords: (use any pressure group name)

Further information on trade unions can be found in the section on 'Law in the workplace' in *The Citizen and the Law* (p.10–11).

Lobbying the government (p. 22)

Aim: To explore the role of lobbyists.

Students could role-play a scene from a television current affairs programme in which an interviewer chairs a discussion between two people, one of whom supports the current lobbying system, while the other thinks it needs to be more tightly controlled.

(SEARCH) Keywords: lobbying + parliament

Spin doctors (p. 23)

Aim: To examine what a spin doctor does.

Copymaster 10: Spot the spin contains a newspaper article that illustrates how spin doctors attempt to manipulate the media, and asks students to detect the spin in other news stories. Media bias is also explored in the section on 'Reporting the news' in *Global Concerns* (p.21).

Students could imagine that they are a teacher with responsibility for liaising with the press. There has been an incident in which half of the fifth year refused to attend a lesson because one of them has been excluded from it, for allegedly threatening the teacher. The local newspaper has heard that there has been a strike at the school and has sent a reporter to cover the story. Draft the statement that the teacher issues, giving the story a spin that suggests it was a very minor incident.

Local government in the United Kingdom (pp. 24–25)

Aim: To explain the organisation and functions of local councils.

Copymaster 11: Researching local government asks students to find out about how local government operates in their area. You could also encourage pupils not only to investigate the status quo but also any current proposals for change, such as the introduction of a directly elected mayor in their areas.

The European Union (pp. 26–27)
How the European Union is run (pp. 28–29)

Aim: To explain what the European Union is, how it is organised and Britain's relationship with it.

Students could share their views on the suggestion that there should be greater integration and that the European Union should aim to develop into a federation of states, following the German model. Up-to-date information about the European Union can be obtained on the Internet from the European Parliament's website http://www.europarl.eu.int and from the following addresses: Information Section, European Commission, 8 Storey's Gate, Westminster, London SW1P 3AT; European Parliament Information Office, 2 Queen Anne's Gate, London SW1H 9AA. The European Commission produces a CD-ROM *Hello Europe:A youth guide to Europe and the European Union.*

International politics (p. 30–31)

Aim: To explain the organisation and functions of the United Nations and the Commonwealth; to look at three countries with non-democratic systems of government.

A more detailed examination of the United Nations and its role in world affairs is contained in *Global Concerns* (pp. 4–7).

Students could imagine that they live in a Commonwealth country where a referendum is being held to decide whether the country should leave the Commonwealth. They should write a statement saying why they think the country should either leave or stay in the Commonwealth.

Copymaster 12: How well do you know Britain's government? is a multiple choice test on the information given in the book. The correct answers are: 1c 2b 3a 4a 5c 6b 7b 8a 9c 10b 11b 12b 13a 14c 15b 16c 17a 18c 19c 20a.

(SEARCH) Keywords: Commonwealth, Empire

The Citizen and the Law

Why do we need laws? (p. 1)

Aim: To explain why we have laws and how laws are made.

Copymaster 13: What do you think about the law? is designed to help students clarify their opinions by thinking about and discussing various statements about the law. As a further activity, groups could imagine they were stranded on a desert island with 200 other people; what are the ten key laws they would try to persuade the group to make?

Civil law and criminal law (pp. 2–3)

Aim: To explain the divisions of the law and the structure of the civil courts and criminal courts systems.

As a follow-up activity, students could look at newspapers to find reports of current law cases, and sort them into criminal and civil law cases.

SEARCH Keywords: court, magistrate

Children and the law (pp. 4–5)

Aim: To examine laws that affect young people.

This topic is also dealt with in the section on children's rights in *Human Rights* (pp.6–9). *Copymaster 14: Time for a change? The child labour laws* presents a newspaper article for discussion. Students are then asked to state what they think the child employment laws should be in a letter to their MP.

Neighbours and the law (pp. 6–7)

Aim: To explore neighbours' rights and responsibilities and how disputes can be settled.

As a follow-up to the discussion activity on page 7, students in pairs can choose one of the situations and role-play a scene in which the two neighbours discuss the issue. Alternatively, groups could role-play the scene in a county court in which a judge hears a case involving a dispute between two neighbours.

Consumers and the law (pp. 8–9)

Aim: To explain how the law protects consumers' rights.

Copymaster 15: Your rights as a consumer presents four case studies for the students to discuss. Their rights are as follows: a) Linda is legally entitled to an exchange or a refund, but she probably won't be able to get one because she has no proof of purchase; b) Steve is entitled to a refund, because clearly the shoes were not fit for the purpose for which they were sold; c) Winston is entitled to a refund as the Sale of Goods Act applies also to goods bought in a sale. Chris is entitled to a refund; d) legally Ann was right, but it is probably not worth the trouble of taking the shop to court to prove that she was. Factsheets and leaflets containing detailed information on consumer rights can be obtained from The Office of Fair Trading, PO Box 366, Hayes UB3 1XB website: www.oft.gov.uk

SEARCH Keywords: consumer + association

Law in the workplace (pp. 10–11)

Aim: To explain employees' legal rights.

Students could carry out a survey about trade unions and people's attitudes towards them. Two copymasters that can be used for this purpose can be found in *Issues 4: Teacher's Resources* (Collins Educational). Further information about trade unions can be obtained from the TUC, Congress House, Great Russell Street, London WC1B 3LS website www.tuc.org.uk

Equal rights (pp. 12–13)

Aim: To examine the laws relating to racial discrimination, sexual discrimination and disability discrimination.

Equal rights are also dealt with in *Human Rights*, which has sections on race discrimination (p.25), the rights of women (pp.26–27), the rights of people with disabilities (pp.30–31) and homosexual discrimination (pp.22–23). *Copymaster 16: Sexual equality and the law* uses two contrasting newspaper articles. Students can discuss the sex discrimination laws and then write a newspaper editorial, expressing their views on them. Further information about sex discrimination and the law can be obtained on the Internet at the Equal Opportunities Commission website http://www.eoc.org.uk or from the Publicity Department, Equal Opportunities Commission, Overseas House, Quay Street, Manchester M3 3HN.

Your personal life (pp. 14–15)

Aim: To explain the laws concerning birth, marriage and death.

Copymaster 17: The law and your personal life

consists of ten suggestions for changes to the law for the students to consider individually, then in groups. A further discussion activity could be developed on the subject of 'cohabitation contracts' – contracts between unmarried couples, who have decided to live together, and who wish to make arrangements for their property and possessions in the event of them splitting up or one of them dying. What do they think of the idea of such contracts? Should they also include agreements about child care duties and about care arrangements for other dependent relatives, such as elderly parents? Should such contracts remain legally binding even if the couple subsequently get married?

Crime (pp. 16–17)

Aim: To explore what is a crime, how much crime there is and what causes it, and to examine the law on drugs.

After discussing their view on the drugs laws, students could write either a newspaper editorial or a letter to a newspaper expressing their opinions. Students can follow up the issues raised on page 17 by drawing up a questionnaire and surveying attitudes and opinions on why there is so much crime and why young people commit crimes. Groups can then role-play a television discussion in which a panel of people express different views on what causes crime and on the best ways to prevent crime.

(SEARCH) Keywords: neighbourhood + watch

Copymaster 18: How can we reduce crime? presents ten suggestions of ways to reduce crime for the students to discuss in groups before writing their own views on how to reduce crime.

The police and their powers (pp. 18–19)

Aim: To examine the role of the police and their powers.

After discussing why we have a police force, students could talk about ways that the public can help the police by taking crime prevention measures and participating in schemes, such as Neighbourhood Watch. They could also discuss the role of private security firms and what the distinction is between such firms and groups of vigilantes.

Copymaster 19: The Police and you is designed to test students' knowledge of the information about police powers and an individual's rights given on these pages. Students could also carry out a survey of people's attitudes towards the police by drawing up a questionnaire to ask people what they think of the police. Encourage them to give the questionnaire to people of different ages, to put the data they collect onto a computer and to analyse it to see whether there is any difference in the attitudes of different age-groups towards the police. You could then contact the local police and arrange for the community liaison officer to visit the class, to talk about police work and what it means to be a police officer, and to discuss the role of the police in our society.

(SEARCH) Keywords: liberty + arrest

The criminal courts 1 – the crown courts (pp. 20–21)

Aim: To explain what happens in crown courts.

Students could discuss how judges are appointed and suggest ways in which the public might be more involved in their appointment. *Copymaster 20: What sentences would you give?* is a sentencing activity, putting the students in the position of the magistrate or judge in having to decide what sentences to give to ten people convicted of a range of different offences. Students could then write their views on what they think the main purpose of punishments should be.

(SEARCH) Keywords: crown + prosecution + service, magistrate, youth + court

The criminal courts 2 – magistrates' courts and youth justice (pp. 22–23)

Aim: To explain what happens in magistrates' courts and youth courts and what sentences can be given to young offenders.

Copymaster 21: In the dock: a case study provides background material for a typical youth justice situation, for students to discuss and perform a role play. Students could then imagine that they were observing the trial, and write a letter to a friend explaining the procedure in the magistrates' court and what the outcome of the trial was.

Prisons (pp. 24–25)

Aim: To provide information on prisons and life in prison.

Copymaster 22: Young Offenders – the need for a different approach? presents three newspaper articles about the treatment of young offenders, two of which focus on the suitability of prison as a punishment for young people, while the third describes a 'restorative justice' project in which young offenders have to meet and repay their victims. Students are then asked to discuss what they think is the most effective way of punishing young offenders.

Further information on prisons, prisoners' rights and alternatives to prison can be obtained by contacting NACRO (National Council for the Care and Resettlement of Offenders), 169 Clapham Road, London SW9 0PU and the Prison Reform Trust e-mail address: prt@prisonreform.demon.co.uk

Road traffic laws (pp. 26–27)

Aim: To explain the laws relating to owning and driving motor vehicles.

Copymaster 23: The road traffic laws is designed to test students' knowledge of the information about driving and motor vehicles given on these pages. The answers are: 1. False 2. False 3. True 4. False (Note: The law does not oblige you to wear a safety helmet when riding a bicycle.) 5. False 6. True 7. False 8. True 9. True 10. False. Students can then work in groups and use the information on these pages to design and write a leaflet for young people – *What you need to know about the road traffic laws* – using an appropriate desktop publishing program to produce it.

SEARCH Keywords: AA, RAC, ROSPA

Environmental law (pp. 28/29)

Aim: To examine the laws that deal with conservation of the countryside, control of pollution and protection of wildlife.

Students could research what new environmental laws are currently under discussion by contacting the local MP. They could then compare what is being done with what environmental pressure groups would like to see done. Information can be obtained from the Internet by visiting the websites of organisations, such as Friends of the Earth at http://www.foe.org.uk and Greenpeace at http://www.greenpeace.org.uk They could then select an issue and produce a detailed statement explaining why environmentalists are concerned about it and why they think new legislation is needed.

SEARCH Keywords: RSPB, environment + agency, Greenpeace

Technology and the law (p. 30)

Aim: To explain laws relating to computer use and to developments in genetic engineering.

Students can use their ICT skills to research the details of the Data Protection Acts of 1984 and 1998 to answer such questions as: How do the Data Protection Acts try to protect you? What rights do they give you? How can you find out who keeps what data? How can you find out what data is held about you? What can you do if the data about you is incorrect? Groups can then prepare a short public information item for radio or television explaining the purpose of the Acts and how to go about finding who is holding data about you and what that data is. Information can be obtained from the Office of the Data Protection Registrar (Wyciffe House, Water Lane, Wilmslow, Cheshire SK9 5AF) e-mail data@wycliffe.demon.co.uk website www.open.gov.uk/dpr/dprhome.htm

Further details of concerns about the Internet can be found in the section 'Problems of the Internet' in *Global Concerns* (page 23). Students could initiate an on-line debate on whether further laws are needed either to control the information that is put on the Internet or to regulate cloning. Details of how to organise an on-line debate are provided on Copymaster 7.

Getting help and advice (p. 31)

Aim: To provide information about the legal profession and how to obtain legal advice.

You could invite a local solicitor to answer questions about the work they do and how they can help people. Students could follow up the visit by writing an article for a teenage magazine, or preparing a factsheet on how to obtain legal help and advice. *Copymaster 24: You and the law* aims to test the knowledge that students have gained from the book by presenting ten situations and asking them what the law is and what they should do in each case. They can then check their answers by looking up the information on the relevant pages in the student's book.

SEARCH Keywords: legal + aid, CAB

Human Rights

What are human rights? (pp. 1–2)

Aim: To explain what human rights are and how they are defined in the United Nations Declaration of Human Rights.

As the UN Declaration of Human Rights is the subject of much of the first unit and is referred to throughout the student's book, *Copymaster 25: The UN Declaration of Human Rights* summarises each article for the students to keep in their files for reference. As a follow-up, you can discuss how throughout history there have been examples of people who have sacrificed their lives or their freedom in the struggle to establish rights that are now considered fundamental, e.g. martyrs who have been prepared to die rather than give up their right to freedom of religious expression; campaigners for civil rights in totalitarian states. Discuss what the pupils consider to be justifiable tactics for human rights campaigners to use in the struggle for their rights. Are there any circumstances in which they feel campaigners might be justified in abandoning peaceful protest and resorting to the use of force?

(SEARCH) Keywords: suffragettes, civil + rights + movement

The time for action (p. 3)

Aim: To explore the actions that can be taken against countries where human rights abuses are occurring.

Ask pupils to write a statement saying what action they think the international community should take against a country in which a government is abusing the human rights of large sections of the population. Get them to read each other's statements and share their ideas in a group discussion.

(SEARCH) Keywords: human + rights + watch

Human rights in Europe (pp. 4–5)

Aim: To explain what the European Convention on Human Rights contains and how human rights are protected in EU countries.

The European Convention on Human Rights has been incorporated into British law in the Human Rights Act 1998, which comes into force in 2000. With regard to the government's failure to set up an integrated human rights commission, it should be pointed out that a disabled rights commission for the UK, and a human rights commission for Northern Ireland (but not the rest of the UK) are now being set up.

Children's rights at home and abroad/ The UN Convention on the Rights of the Child/ Child slavery (pp. 6–9)

Aim: To explain what rights children have and to look at how far these rights are respected in the UK and globally.

Copymaster 26: The rights of young adults presents extracts from letters written by young adults in six different countries. Each of the letters raises issues about what rights young adults have in their country for the students to discuss. Additional information relevant to this topic can be found in the section 'Children and the law' on pages 4–5 of *The Citizen and the Law*.

A range of materials which can be used in conjunction with these pages:

● A video entitled 'The Rights of the Child', are available from UNICEF, Unit 1, Rignals Lane, Chelmsford, Essex CM2 8TU.

● A video about child workers in India, Pakistan and Bangladesh, *Angels with Dirty Faces,* can be hired from CAFOD, who have also published a Child Labour factsheet. CAFOD also run education days focussing on the issue of child labour. Full details are available from CAFOD, Romero House, Stockwell Road, London SW9 9TY (e-mail: hqcafod@cafod.org.uk).

Up-to-date information on legislation which affects children and young people can also be obtained from The Children's Legal Centre, University of Essex, Wivenhoe Park, Colchester, Essex CO4 3SQ. Their Internet home page address is: http://www2.essex.ac.uk/clc An international organisation which campaigns to protect the rights of the child is: Anti-Slavery International (AIS), The Stableyard, Broomgrove Road, London SW9 9TL e-mail antislavery@gn.apc.org

Freedom of expression (pp. 10–11)

Aim: To explore two issues connected with freedom of religious belief – blasphemy and euthanasia.

Students could role-play a discussion during a television current affairs programme in which an invited panel of people with differing opinions discuss the blasphemy laws and how appropriate they are in a modern multicultural society. They could then write a short statement giving their views on whether the law should be changed in any way.

Copymaster 27: The right to die presents a number of case studies which raise key questions in order to help pupils understand the arguments for and against euthanasia. Detailed statements of the opposing viewpoints can be obtained on the Internet, for example from The Voluntary Euthanasia Society's home page http://www.ves.org.uk or by writing to The Voluntary Euthanasia Society, 13 Prince of Wales Terrace, London W8 5PG and The Human Rights Society, Mariners Yard, Cley, Holt, Norfolk NR25 7RX.

Copymaster 28: What do you think about freedom of expression? lists ten views on issues concerning freedom of expression for students to think about on their own and then discuss in groups.

Torture, the death penalty and the right to a fair trial (pp. 12–13)

Aim: To explore how the right to freedom from torture, the right to life and the right to a fair trial are often abused when freedom of expression is restricted.

Copymaster 29: Prisoners of conscience presents Amnesty International's letter-writing campaign as a springboard for the students' own letter-writing. A current prisoner of conscience could, of course, be substituted for the invented case here. Information can be obtained from the Amnesty International website http://www.amnesty.org.uk or by writing to Amnesty Youth Action at Amnesty International UK, 99–109 Roseberry Avenue, London EC1R 4RE. *Copymaster 30: Capital punishment* consists of a series of statements presenting the arguments for and against the death penalty. After debating the issue, you could ask students to imagine that there is going to be a vote in Parliament on a proposal to reintroduce the death penalty for certain crimes. Ask them to write a letter to their MP saying which way they want the MP to vote.

Economic rights (pp. 14–15)

Aim: To discuss the right to work and workers' rights.

Point out that there are a number of people who

choose not to work and how such people are often stereotyped as scroungers in a society where the current policy is to try to link welfare payments to schemes that will enable people to find jobs. Debate the idea that people have a right to opt out of employment and not to work if they do not want to do so.

SEARCH Keywords: low + pay + unit

Immigrants, refugees and asylum seekers (pp. 16–17)

Aim: To discuss the rights of immigrants, refugees and asylum seekers.

Copymaster 31: Refugees – what are the facts? is designed to test students' knowledge and prejudices about refugees in the UK. (Numbers 2, 5, 6 and 10 are false; the rest are true.) Students could also imagine that they are all members of the same political party and that they have been given the task of drafting their party's policy on refugees. Groups can take it in turns to present the policy, sharing their views in a class discussion. Further work on refugees can be developed using materials produced by The Refugee Council, 3 Bondway, London SW8 1SJ website: www.refugeecouncil.org.uk These include leaflets and videos and *Refugees – We Left Because We Had To,* a book containing a wide range of suggestions for classroom activities. A booklet in which young refugees and minority students tell their stories – *Forging New Identities* – is available from Minority Rights Group International, 379 Brixton Road, London SW9 7DE. The Minority Rights website is: www.minorityrights.org

Social rights/ The basic needs for survival (pp. 18–21)

Aim: To explore people's rights to security, a home and an adequate standard of living, examining the issues of poverty, homelessness, malnutrition and access to clean water.

Many of the poorest people in Britain are older people: students could work in groups to research the needs of older people and how far they are being adequately met. They can report their findings in a class discussion on whether or not older people are being denied their social rights. Useful sources of information about older people in the UK can be found on the Internet at Age Concern's website: http://www.age.org.uk

and Help the Aged's website: http://www.helptheaged.org.uk or by writing to Age Information Department, Age Concern England, Astral House, 1268 London Road, London SW16 4ER and Help the Aged, St James Walk, Clerkenwell Green, London EC1R 0BH. Information and suggestions for activities on housing and homelessness can be obtained in materials produced by organisations such as Shelter, 88 Old Street, London EC1V 9HU; Crisis, 1st Floor, Challenger House, 42 Adler Street, London E1 1EE; CHAS (The Catholic Housing Aid Society) 209 Old Marylebone Road, London NW1 5QT. Their Internet home page addresses are: Shelter http://www.shelter.org.uk and Crisis http://www.crisis.org.uk

Copymaster 32: Travellers' rights consists of two newspaper articles about travellers for students to study and discuss. They raise issues concerning the rights of travellers to choose not to have a fixed abode and to lead a lifestyle that is different from that of most people. As a follow-up to pages 20–21, ask groups of students to find out about the long-term development programmes aimed at supplying food and clean water supported by organisations such as Oxfam, Water Aid, Christian Aid, The Catholic Agency for Overseas Development (CAFOD) and Muslim Aid. Information on water issues can be obtained from Water Aid, Prince Consort House, 27-29 Albert Embankment, London SE1 7UB or their website http://www.wateraid.org.uk

Civil rights in the UK – homosexual discrimination (pp. 22–23)

Aim: To consider the rights of homosexuals.

Information about homosexuals and their rights can be obtained from The Campaign for Homosexual Equality, P.O.Box 342, London WC1X 0DU.

Civil rights – the USA compared with the UK (pp. 24–25)

Aim: To compare the right of US citizens to bear arms with the UK's gun control laws, and to examine racism and human rights issues in the USA and the UK.

Racial discrimination is also dealt with on page 12 of *The Citizen and the Law* which gives details of the Race Relations Act 1976 and what it outlaws. *Copymaster 33: Racism* presents for discussion five cases which raise key issues about racism.

Copymaster 34: How can we improve race relations? is a ranking activity. Students are asked to rank twelve suggestions of how to improve race relations in order of effectiveness, then to compare their views in a group discussion. Factsheets and information on racism and race relations can be found on the website of the Commission for Racial Equality: www.cre.gov.uk

The rights of women (pp. 26-27)

Aim: To explore equal opportunities issues and sexual discrimination in the UK.

Details of the Sex Discrimination Acts of 1975 and 1986 and of the Equal Pay Act 1970 can be found on page 13 of *The Citizen and the Law*.

(SEARCH) Keywords: Fawcett + society, equal + opportunities

The right to life (pp. 28–29)

Aim: To present information on abortion and to explore different attitudes towards abortion.

Further materials presenting the opposing arguments on abortion can be obtained from LIFE, Life House, Newbold Terrace, Leamington Spa CV32 4EA and Pro-Choice Alliance, 27-35 Mortimer Street, London W1N 7RJ.

The rights of the disabled (pp. 30–31)

Aim: To define disability and explore the rights of people with disabilities.

Copymaster 35: Facilities for disabled people: a survey consists of a questionnaire which can be used by students to find out whether public buildings in their area are equipped with facilities that enable people with disabilities to participate fully in the community. As a follow-up, students could write a letter to their local paper either praising or criticising the local community for the way it provides access for people with disabilities. Information on disability rights issues can be obtained from the Royal Association for Disability and Rehabilitation (RADAR), 12 City Forum, 250 City Road, London EC1V 8AF and their website www.radar.org.uk

Copymaster 36: Do you know your rights? is a multiple choice test on the information given in the book. The answers are: 1c 2c 3c 4b 5a 6a 7c 8b 9a 10c 11c 12c 13c 14c 15c 16c 17b 18a 19c 20a.

Global Concerns

What is power? (p. 1)

Aim: To explain the different kinds of power and where power is concentrated in the world today.

As a follow-up, you can discuss how where political power lies in a state depends on a country's system of government. Explain that in a democracy it lies ultimately with all the citizens, while in a totalitarian state it lies with the sole political party and in a dictatorship it is in the hands of one person. Examples of different types of political systems can be found in *Democracy in Action* (pp.30–31).

What is globalisation? (pp. 2–3)

Aim: To explain what globilisation is, what has caused it and what its effects are on the distribution of power.

A key issue to focus on during the discussion of the impact of globalisation is the question of accountability. Students could use the Internet to find out about the World Development Movement, 25 Beehive Place, London SW9 7QR and the growing power of transnational corporations, by visiting their home page: http://www.wdm.org.uk

The United Nations (pp. 4–5)

Aim: To describe how the United Nations is organised and the work of some of its main agencies and commissions.

To understand the background to the establishment of the United Nations students could research the setting up of the League of Nations.

(SEARCH) Keywords: League + nations; United + nations.

The United Nations Security Council (pp. 6–7)

Aim: To examine the composition and functions of the UN Security Council and explore how effective it has been in resolving conflicts and keeping the peace.

Copymaster 37: The UN Security Council(1) and *Copymaster 38: The UN Security Council (2)* contain a role-play, with students representing countries on the UN Security Council, debating a resolution on imposing economic sanctions on Russia, in a situation based on the 1999/2000 war in Chechnya. Country cards should be cut out from Copymaster 38 and distributed amongst the students. Each student should have one card only and not look at anyone else's card at any time. Make sure that at least five students undertake this activity and that the cards for the permanent members of the UN Security Council are distributed first. Emphasise the importance of the veto that the permanent members have when the resolution comes to a final vote. The goal of this activity is to show how a set of negotiations can fail, even when a majority of countries are in favour of a course of action, due to a veto. As an alternative, you could then remove the veto and allow a vote by a simple majority, to demonstrate how reform of the UN Security Council might work.

A second exercise is contained on Copymaster 37. Students can draft a presentation on behalf of an organisation interested in the conflict and present information to other students, who can then ask questions. If you wish to involve the entire class, the two activites can be combined. 12 students can role-play the UN Security Council, which takes evidence, and the other students can draft and then make presentations on behalf of international organisations. This activity can be used as a springboard for discussion on a variety of subjects, including refugees, landmines, and enforcing human rights.

(SEARCH) Keywords: UN + Security + Council, Chechnya

Third World Debt (pp. 8–9)

Aim: To explain what has caused Third World Debt and to examine the problems arising from it.

Copymaster 39: Fair Trade contains an article 'We're going bananas', adapted from the New Internationalist magazine. This provides a case study of how the banana industry contributes to third world debt, poverty and environmental problems. Students are asked to consider the problems of the banana industry and how fair trade might be achieved. Students could undertake a research project by visiting the Jubilee 2000 website www.jubilee2000uk.org – to see what stage developed countries have reached in writing off third world debts to Less Developed Countries.

Global trade and international finance (pp. 10–11)

Aim: To explain what exchange rates are, the effects currency speculation can have on economies and what the Tobin tax would do.

Students could use the Internet to research the arguments for and against joining a single currency.

(SEARCH) Keywords: Business + sterling, Britain + in + Europe

They could also contact War on Want, 37–39 Great Guildford Street, London SE1 0YU to get an update on War on Want's campaign for the Tobin tax.

Population (pp. 12–13)

Aim: To explain the causes and implications of population growth and to examine the issue of population control.

Copymaster 40: Population matters presents ten statements asking the students to decide which are true and which are false. 1, 3, 9 and 10 are false; the rest are true.

Further information on population issues including student packs and a software pack can be obtained from Population Concern, 178–202 Great Portland Street, London W1N 5TB.

World hunger (pp. 14–15)

Aim: To investigate the relative merits of changing farming methods, changing land use and growing genetically modified crops as ways of solving the problem of food shortage.

Copymaster 41: World hunger presents ten statements of actions that could be taken to help to solve the problem of world hunger. Students are asked to rank them in order of effectiveness, then to share their views in a class discussion.

(SEARCH) Keywords: GM + food, intensive + farming

Poverty (pp. 16–17)

Aim: To explain why some countries are poor and the relationship between education and poverty; to compare poverty in developed and developing countries.

Students could research how colonisation by developed countries has led to poverty in many parts of the world today. A video, 'Poverty Answering Back, distributed by Oxfam, provides eight first-hand accounts of people living in poverty, as well as an analysis of poverty in a global context. *Copymaster 42: Education for all* consists of an article from *The Guardian* which explains how poverty and a lack of education are closely interlinked. Students are asked to imagine the disadvantages illiteracy creates. Students could then discuss what it would be like in a school in a poverty-stricken developing country.

World Health (pp. 18–19)

Aim: To examine ways of improving health in the developing world; to discuss the problems of the overuse of antibiotics and of the AIDS epidemic.

Copymaster 43: Health Resources contains an article adapted from *The Daily Telegraph*, examining how older people are discriminated against in the NHS. This is used as a start for discussion activities about rationing healthcare. Students could discuss whether an immunisation for flu, launched late in 1999, should be made available to their own age-group, babies, and elderly persons, free of charge. Details of other resources on these topics are available on the database produced by the Health Education Authority at http://healthpromis.hea.org.uk

The media (pp. 20–21)

Aim: To examine issues of media ownership and media control.

Copymaster 44: A free media? contains an article by Project Censored, an organisation that examines which news stories were not reported each year. Students are asked to think about who benefits from censorship. They could then visit Project Censored's website at www.sonoma.edu/ProjectCensored for an up-to-date list of the top 25 stories which were not reported each year and consider why these stories were not reported.

The Internet (pp. 22–23)

Aim: To explore the development of the Internet and to examine its various problems.

Copymaster 45: Using the Cool Planet website shows how the Internet can be used constructively, with a guide to Cool Planet, a website on global issues maintained by Oxfam. Cool Planet can be found at *www.oxfam.org.uk/coolplanet/*

Students are first asked to produce a short summary of Oxfam's work in one country and to compare their findings with other countries researched by other students. A second activity asks students to complete a multiple choice questionnaire on the issue of developing world aid. Finally, students can examine the issues of recycling and fair trade. The website contains detailed teachers' notes. It is recommended that teachers examine the website themselves before starting these activities, to see what material has been updated.

Copymaster 46: Internet issues concentrates on the negative aspects of the Internet, containing two articles that examine the issues of the right to privacy, child pornography and computer hacking. Students are asked to debate these issues and to discuss what limits they would place on Internet access at home if they were parents with children.

The arms trade (pp. 24–25)

Aim: To examine the UK's involvement in the arms trade and to explore what is meant by an ethical foreign policy.

Copymaster 47: Ethical arms presents ten statements about the ethical implications of trading in arms, for students to agree/disagree with, before drafting a letter to their local MP on one of these issues. Groups could be asked to imagine that they are government advisers who have been asked to draw up a set of guidelines for an ethical foreign policy that will determine Britain's relationships with countries where human rights are being abused. Their task is to state the principles on which the ethical foreign policy will be based. Information about the arms trade can be obtained from Campaign Against Arms Trade (CAAT), 11 Goodwin Street, London N4 3HQ www.caat.demon.co.uk.

Weapons of mass destruction (pp. 26–27)

Aim: To explain how weapons of mass destruction threaten world peace; to discuss the arguments for nuclear disarmament and the banning of landmines.

Students could contact the Campaign for Nuclear Disarmament to explore the problems of nuclear proliferation in countries such as North Korea, Iraq and Israel. Up-to-date information about the banning of landmines can be obtained from the UK Working Group on Landmines, the UK arm of the International Campaign to Ban Landmines, 601 Holloway Road, London N19 4Dj E-mail: ukwglm@msn.com

The environment (pp. 28–29)

Aim: To explain the causes and effects of global warming and to examine ways of reducing it.

Students could write an information leaflet for the general public on what steps they could take locally to help reduce fossil fuel emissions. They could then compare their materials with those produced by Greenpeace www.greenpeace.org.uk Students could also contact their local council to see what steps they are taking as part of the Agenda 21 environmental programme.

Species extinction and deforestation (p. 30)

Aim: To explain what causes species extinction, deforestation, and what is meant by sustainable forestry.

Students could contact the World Wide Fund for Nature to see which species are most under threat, and what can be done to protect them. Contact WWF UK Panda House, Weyside Park, Godalming, Surrey GU7 1XR Tel: 01483 426444 website:www.wwf-uk.org Friends of the Earth also have a website: www.foe.co.uk

Students could contact the pressure group Survival, 11-15 Emerald Street, London, WC1N 3QL website www.survival-international.org to examine why tribes in South America depend on rainforests to survive, and what other pressures exist that cause deforestation.

The future of our environment (p. 31)

Aim: To examine the view that the solution to the world's environmental problems lies in accepting collective responsibility and acting co-operatively.

Students could contact the Department for the Environment, Transport and the Regions to find out what is being done to ensure that the United Kingdom meets the targets set in the Rio and Kyoto Agreements to protect the environment.

Copymaster 48:What do you know about the world? is a multiple choice test on the information given in the book. The answers are: 1c 2a 3b 4c 5b 6b 7c 8b 9c 10c 11b 12b 13b 14c 15a 16a 17b 18b 19b 20a.

Setting up a school council

Look at the flowchart below, which takes you through the stages of writing a constitution for your school council. An example is given on the right.

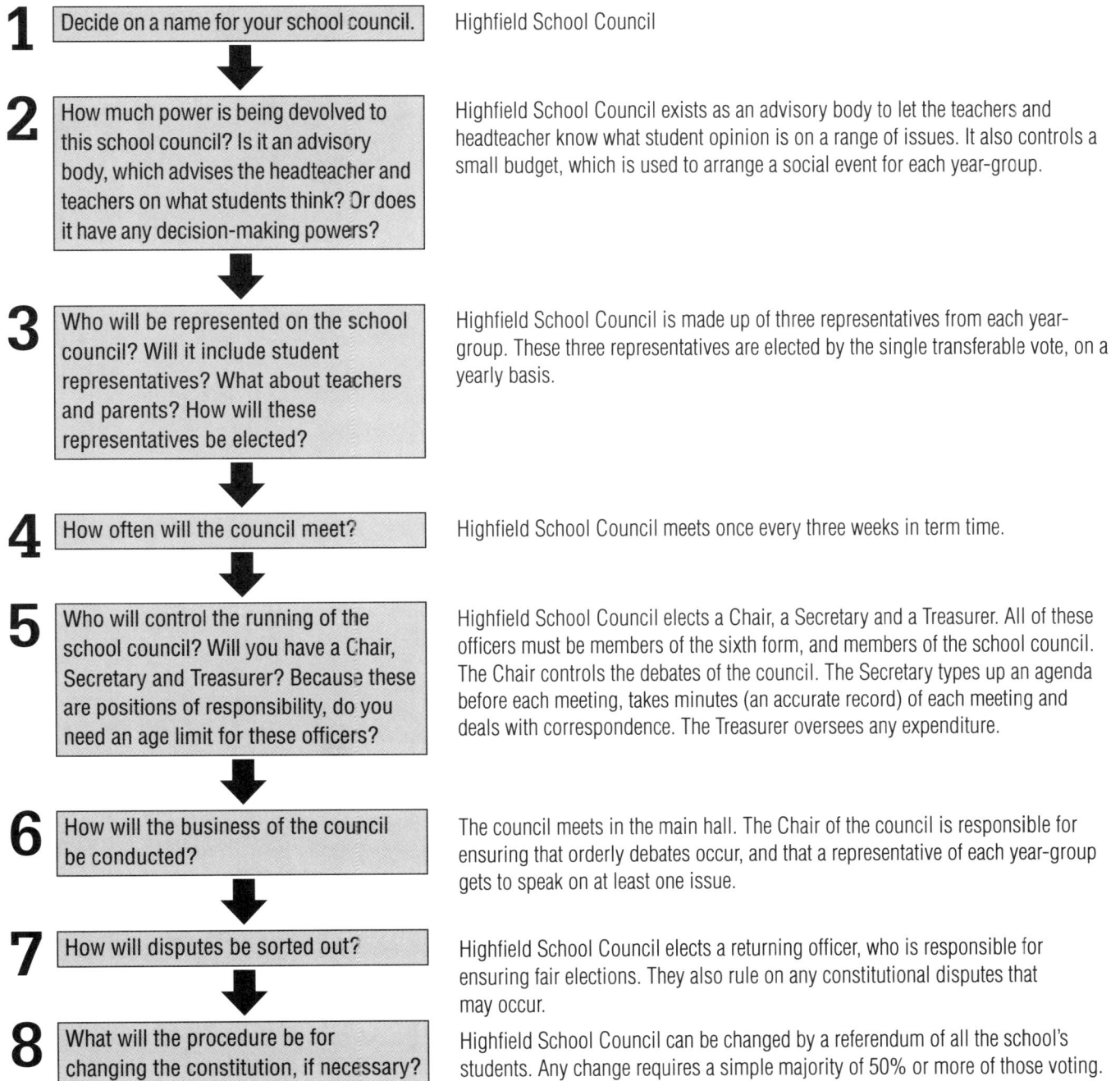

1 | Decide on a name for your school council.

Highfield School Council

2 | How much power is being devolved to this school council? Is it an advisory body, which advises the headteacher and teachers on what students think? Or does it have any decision-making powers?

Highfield School Council exists as an advisory body to let the teachers and headteacher know what student opinion is on a range of issues. It also controls a small budget, which is used to arrange a social event for each year-group.

3 | Who will be represented on the school council? Will it include student representatives? What about teachers and parents? How will these representatives be elected?

Highfield School Council is made up of three representatives from each year-group. These three representatives are elected by the single transferable vote, on a yearly basis.

4 | How often will the council meet?

Highfield School Council meets once every three weeks in term time.

5 | Who will control the running of the school council? Will you have a Chair, Secretary and Treasurer? Because these are positions of responsibility, do you need an age limit for these officers?

Highfield School Council elects a Chair, a Secretary and a Treasurer. All of these officers must be members of the sixth form, and members of the school council. The Chair controls the debates of the council. The Secretary types up an agenda before each meeting, takes minutes (an accurate record) of each meeting and deals with correspondence. The Treasurer oversees any expenditure.

6 | How will the business of the council be conducted?

The council meets in the main hall. The Chair of the council is responsible for ensuring that orderly debates occur, and that a representative of each year-group gets to speak on at least one issue.

7 | How will disputes be sorted out?

Highfield School Council elects a returning officer, who is responsible for ensuring fair elections. They also rule on any constitutional disputes that may occur.

8 | What will the procedure be for changing the constitution, if necessary?

Highfield School Council can be changed by a referendum of all the school's students. Any change requires a simple majority of 50% or more of those voting.

In groups ⟩ Imagine that you were setting up a school council for your school. Use the above guidelines to draft a short constitution.

As a class ⟩ Compare your constitutions, on a point-by-point basis. How and why do they differ?

Citizenship in Focus Teacher's Resources

The monarchy – what are the facts?

Here are twelve statements about the monarchy. Discuss with a partner, which ones are true and which ones are false. Put a tick in the correct box after each statement.

		TRUE	FALSE
1	The monarch is the head of state in Britain.	☐	☐
2	The monarch attends cabinet meetings.	☐	☐
3	All new laws made by Parliament have to be approved by the monarch.	☐	☐
4	The monarch's powers are set out in the UK's written constitution.	☐	☐
5	Each session of Parliament is opened by the monarch.	☐	☐
6	The monarchy costs the British taxpayer over £1.3 billion per year.	☐	☐
7	The monarch decides which people are to be made life peers.	☐	☐
8	The monarch is the spiritual head of the Church of England.	☐	☐
9	Members of the royal family are expected to belong to a political party.	☐	☐
10	Britain has always been a constitutional monarchy.	☐	☐
11	The head of the monarchy, the Queen, is head of the Commonwealth.	☐	☐
12	A majority of people in the United Kingdom would like to abolish the monarchy.	☐	☐

As a class Hold a debate on the following motion: *This house believes that the monarchy should be reformed, but not abolished.*

How to hold a debate

Glossary

Look at the rules of debating given below. There is a glossary on the right to help you with some of the terms.

1 The **Chair** opens the meeting, and checks who is present and who is able to vote at the meeting.

2 The Chair either reads out the **motion** or asks the **proposer** to do so.

3 The proposer speaks in favour of the motion.

4 The **opposer** speaks against the motion.

5 Each of the **seconders** then speaks – one for, and then one against the motion.

6 If there are any **amendments**, the proposer of each amendment reads it out, followed by an opposer of each amendment, who speaks against.

7 The Chair declares the motion 'open to the floor'. This means that anyone in the audience may now speak, either for or against the motion, or for or against an amendment. Anyone who wishes to speak raises their hand, and the Chair asks them to speak in turn.

8 After a balanced debate has occurred, the Chair invites the main speakers for and against each amendment to give a summary. Each amendment is then voted on.

9 The Chair asks the opposer to give a brief summary of why people should vote against the motion.

10 The Chair asks the proposer to give a brief summary of why people should vote for the motion.

11 A vote is then organised, either in public (with a show of hands), or by a secret ballot. The Chair usually organises this. The result is counted: those in favour of the motion, those against the motion and those who wish to **abstain**.

12 The Chair announces the result of the vote, and declares that the motion is either passed (the house agreed with the motion) or defeated (the house disagreed with the motion).

Chair. The debate is controlled by a person known as the Chair.

Motion. The motion is the viewpoint which people will argue for or against. The motion is presented in a formal way, which begins, 'This house believes that …'.

Proposer. The proposer is usually, but not always, the author of the motion. They begin the debate, speaking in favour of the motion.

Opposer. The opposer speaks against the motion, after the proposer has made their speech.

Seconder. The two seconders are the people who speak after the proposer and opposer: one speaks in favour of the motion, and one against.

Amendment. Amendments may be proposed to the main motion. These change the wording of the motion slightly. Amendments also require proposers and seconders.

Abstain. If you do not vote either for or against the motion, because you cannot make up your mind, or you disagree with both opposing views, you are said to abstain.

As a class

Hold a debate, either on a motion of your choice, or on one of the following motions:

1 This house believes that the United Kingdom should be part of a federal Europe.

2 This house believes that England should have at least eight regional parliaments, which would have similar powers to the Welsh Assembly, to represent the people in different regions of England.

3 This house believes that there should be a national assembly for young people, elected by secondary school students aged between 11 and 17.

Changing the voting system

On your own

Below is a questionnaire on changing the voting system. Use it to determine the views of a group of adults known to you, or members of the public. Try to get at least five people to answer all the questions.

If you are asking members of the public, tell them your name and the name of your school, and say that you are doing a project on current affairs. Always be polite and thank the person you are asking, whether or not they wish to answer your questions.

1 How often do you vote in General Elections?
  A Always, or nearly always ☐
  B Sometimes ☐
  C Never ☐

2 Do you think that the electoral system we have for General Elections is fair?
  A Yes ☐
  B No ☐
  C Don't know ☐

3 Why do you think that?
_____
_____
_____
_____

4 Are you aware that the government is thinking of changing the voting system?
  A Yes ☐
  B No ☐
  C Don't know ☐

5 One of the government's aims is to make the voting system more proportional. In other words, the total number of seats each party won would be closer to the total number of votes cast in the country for each party. Do you think this is a good idea?
  A Yes ☐
  B No ☐
  C Don't know ☐

6 Why do you think that?
_____
_____
_____
_____

7 Are there any other comments you would like to add to what you have already said?
_____
_____
_____
_____

In groups

When you have finished, compare your results with others in your group, to see what you have learnt.

Devolution in the United Kingdom

Use this questionnaire to find out the views of adults on devolution in the United Kingdom. Try to get at least five people to answer all of the questions.

If you are asking members of the public, tell them your name and the name of your school. Tell them that you are doing a project on current affairs. Always be polite and thank the person you are asking, whether or not they want to answer your questions.

1 Do you think devolution or regional government is generally a good idea?
Yes ☐   No ☐   Don't know ☐

2 Scotland now has its own parliament. Do you think there should be an English parliament as well?
Yes ☐   No ☐   Don't know ☐

3 Scotland's parliament has the power to raise or lower taxes, but the Welsh Assembly does not. Do you think this is fair?
Yes ☐   No ☐   Don't know ☐

4 Would you vote if we had elections for a devolved government in this area?
Yes ☐   No ☐   Don't know ☐

5 Do you think coalition governments in the Scottish parliament and the Welsh Assembly are a good idea?
Yes ☐   No ☐   Don't know ☐

6 Why do you think that?
_____
_____
_____

7 Are you aware that London now has its own directly elected mayor?
Yes ☐   No ☐   Don't know ☐

8 The government is thinking that major large cities in England, e.g. Liverpool, should have their own directly elected mayors. Do you think this is a good idea?
Yes ☐   No ☐   Don't know ☐

9 Why do you think that?
_____
_____
_____

10 Are there any other comments you would like to add to what you have already said?
_____
_____
_____
_____
_____

In groups   Compare your answers with three or four other people's. What trends do you begin to notice? Are people enthusiastic about devolution, unenthusiastic or disinterested? Can you explain why?

Citizenship in Focus Teacher's Resources

A revised upper chamber

Read below about the upper chambers of the United States and the United Kingdom.

Name:
The United States Senate

Members:
100 members, two elected from each state of the USA.

System of appointment:
Election by first past the post. One third of the Senate is elected every two years.

Length of service:
Each senator serves for six years.

Key powers:
1 No bill can become law in the USA without Senate approval.
2 The Senate contains a number of key committees which oversee parts of the government, including foreign affairs, the judiciary and defence.
3 The Senate must approve all appointments for ambassadors, cabinet members and senior judges.

Name:
The House of Lords

Members:
26 law lords, 26 bishops and archbishops of the Church of England, over 650 life peers and 91 elected hereditary peers.

System of appointment:
Life peers are appointed by the government. Hereditary peers were elected in 1999.

Length of service:
Life peers sit for life, or until they resign. Elected hereditary peers will sit in the House of Lords until it is fully reformed.

Key powers:
1 Final court of appeal: five of the law lords sit as the final court of appeal in the UK.
2 Secondary chamber which may amend legislation. All bills have to be formally approved by the House of Lords, or may be delayed by up to 12 months by the House. The exception are bills relating to the economy.
3 The House of Lords has a number of parliamentary committees, which may influence the government.

On your own

Construct a table to indicate what you think a future upper chamber for the UK should look like. Use the same headings: Name, Members, System of appointment, Length of service and Key powers.

As a class

Compare your results. Has there been general agreement on any of the issues?

Using the Internet

*Find an on-line discussion group on current affairs that you are interested in joining. Your teacher may be able to suggest some, or you can search for one using the Internet. The **join** command on your computer will allow you to join the discussion group. A teacher or the **help** command on the computer can provide you with assistance if you run into difficulties.*

*When you join the group, you may find that there is a **moderator**. The moderator is the person who makes sure that the rules of the discussion group are followed.*

The diagram below shows how a discussion group works: it is a sample discussion group on the death penalty.

Message no.	Who sent the message	First line of the message
1	Abbas [moderator]	Welcome. Here are the rules of this discussion group …
2	Michaela	Query: does this discussion group include abortion?
3	Abbas	No. I'll find the abortion discussion group for you.
4	Rob	10 reasons why we should have the death penalty …
5	Shaun	Why I disagree with Rob …
6	Rob	Yes, but have you considered the effect on crime …
7	Carole	10 more good reasons for the death penalty …
8	Michaela	Statistics on the death penalty …

In this discussion group the moderator (Abbas) starts the first **thread** of the topic by stating the rules (message 1). A thread is a conversation which develops as messages are posted in the topic.

Rob starts a separate thread with message 4. Shaun comments on Rob's message (message 5), as does Carole (message 7). In the meantime, Rob chooses to add to Shaun's comments (message 6). In this way a conversation gradually builds up. By clicking on each message, it is possible to see what each person has said in detail.

Occasionally a new part of the issue will be debated. For example, Michaela has started a new thread discussing statistics on the death penalty (message 8). Everyone is free both to add to this thread and to continue the discussion of Rob's ten reasons why we should have the death penalty.

Discussion group rules

Be sure to follow all the rules of the discussion group. Common rules are:

1. Everyone should try to stick to the general subject of discussion, as outlined by the moderator.

2. Where someone has a specific question to an individual person, they should e-mail that person privately.

3. No **wibble** (off-topic chatter) is allowed.

4. If someone has a dispute with another member of the group, they should e-mail the moderator, who will deal with it privately.

5. No personal comments, insults or bad language is allowed. Any such comments will be immediately withdrawn by the moderator. Persistent use of such comments will result in that person's access to the group being withdrawn.

6. The moderator's decision is final.

Lobbying in action

Who are Passports for Pets?

Passports for Pets is a pressure group. It was set up in 1994. Passports for Pets has campaigned for a change in Britain's quarantine laws. These laws mean that any cat, dog or rabbit which enters the country must be placed in isolation – quarantine – for six months. These laws were created over a century ago to prevent the spread of rabies.

Why does Passports for Pets want to change the law?

A microchip is inserted under the animal's skin to provide permanent identification, followed by a vaccine against rabies. After a successful blood test, the pet would then be issued with a passport, showing that it was free of rabies and it was safe for the animal to enter the country.

How successful has Passports for Pets been?

Very successful, and it is finally achieving its aims. In March 1999, the government agreed to a pilot scheme using microchips for February 2000. A larger scheme is planned for 2001.

Why are Passports for Pets so successful?

The main strength of Passports for Pets is that it successfully used a variety of different campaign techniques to mobilise public support to lobby the government. These included the following:

- Persuading celebrities, such as Elton John and other groups, like the RSPCA, to support their campaign.

- Running a series of high profile advertisements in the media.

- Organising press conferences and issuing press releases.

- Producing case studies of abuse to animals caused by quarantine.

- Making it easy for members to join – visit their website on http://freespace.virgin.net/passports.forpets

- Involving its members through fund-raising and letter-writing campaigns.

- Keeping in contact with its members through newsletters.

In groups

Study the information (above) and discuss the reasons why Passports for Pets has been so successful.

Do you think UK pressure groups should be given free television airtime on local cable television stations, funded by taxpayers, as already occurs in America? Explain why.

In the United Kingdom, pressure groups are not allowed to declare themselves to be charities if they have political aims. This means that pressure groups such as Passports for Pets have to pay tax. Do you think that this law should be changed? Why? Give reasons for your views.

On your own

Look through the national newspapers and at news stories on television and the Internet. What pressure groups can you see as being successful? Why? What campaign techniques are they using?

Setting up a pressure group

In groups Set up your own pressure group by following the flowchart below.

Choose an issue that you would like to campaign for
Either choose your own issue to campaign for, or use one of the following:
1 Encouraging more young people to vote in your local area in local council elections;
2 Improving community facilities for young people in your local area.

Decide on the aim of your pressure group
For example:
1 Increase the turnout for young people voting in local elections by 10%;
2 Get a new community centre built with leisure facilities for young people.

Choose a name for your pressure group
This should be:
1 Something easy to remember, and that the media will notice;
2 Relevant to the aims you have set for your group.

Think about the constitution of your pressure group
For example:
1 Should there be any restrictions on membership?
   (e.g. do members have to be a certain age?)
2 Will you have a written constitution?

Decide who you need to target to help the cause of your pressure group
For example:
1 All young people, to increase turnout in local elections;
2 The local council, who are in charge of building community centres.

Decide how you will raise money for your pressure group
For example:
1 Will you charge a subscription to be a member of your group?
2 Will you hold fund-raising events?
3 Will you ask companies to sponsor your pressure group?

Decide what campaign techniques to use to gain public support
For example:
1 Demonstrations;
2 Press releases, leaflets and letters to the local papers;
3 The Internet.

If you decide to set new objectives, then look again at the aim of your group.

Decide how you will measure the success of your pressure group
1 When will you decide whether your pressure group has been successful or not?
2 How will you measure this success?
3 If your group has been unsuccessful, will you dissolve it or set new objectives?

25

Spot the spin

Government announces fall in unemployment figures

The government today announced that the rate of growth of unemployment was falling. Commenting on today's figures, the Employment Secretary said, 'I am pleased by this good news – it shows that the battle against unemployment is being successful.'

'After the last 18 years of the opposition party being in power,' he added, 'we are doing very well to be turning this round so fast. We now have the resources, the means and the will to deal with this problem.'

Pressure groups immediately asked the government what it would be doing to create jobs in areas of high unemployment. Sources close to the Prime Minister confirmed that he was looking at different options to create more jobs. 'We are positive that new measures will be announced soon,' a senior government official said.

Using misleading statistics. Although 'the rate of growth of unemployment' is going down, unemployment is still going up, but at a slower rate.

Using the lobby. Senior sources are quoted, rather than the Prime Minister himself. This is known as speaking 'on lobby terms'. The idea is to have a useful news quote, which cannot actually be attributed to anybody. Thus the Prime Minister cannot be held accountable for anything in this news story.

Emphasising the positive. The headline gives a positive spin because it talks about a 'fall in unemployment figures' even though unemployment itself is still rising (see left).

Blaming others. Blaming the previous government for current problems is an example of negative spin.

Using lists of three. This is a useful speechwriting technique which reinforces an idea in an attractive way.

Saying nothing of substance, and promising nothing. The government have promised nothing, but are still presenting themselves in a good light.

On your own

Read the newspaper article above carefully. Then think about the spin-doctoring techniques that are being used (the notes around the article guide you through these).

Now look at recent newspaper stories about politics and current affairs. See if you can identify any examples of spin-doctoring techniques being used.

Writing

Imagine you are a local council spokesperson. There has been a serious pollution accident at a local council landfill site, the first in 15 years. The council's safety record is far better than that of the neighbouring council. While nobody has been seriously injured, some of the local wildlife has had to be treated. There appear to be no long-term effects.

Issue a press release giving details of the incident. Give it the best possible spin.

Researching local government

Below are ten questions for you to answer on local government in your area. (It may take you time to find out some of the information!)

1 What sort of local council governs your local area? Is it:
  A a single metropolitan district council (usually the case if you live in a big city); ☐
  B a district council and a county council; ☐
  C a unitary authority? ☐

(Note: if you have a district and county council, then the following questions apply to your district council.)

2 What is the name of your local council (e.g. Newcastle Metropolitan Borough Council, Cherwell District Council, Torbay Unitary Authority)?
_____

3 How big an area does your local council cover?
_____

4 What are the main services your local council is responsible for?
_____
_____
_____
_____

5 Give the name of one of your local councillors who represents you (this depends on exactly where you live).
_____

6 Briefly describe what the job of this local councillor involves.
_____
_____
_____

7 Does any party have a majority on your local council? If so, which one?
_____

8 How often does your local council have elections?
  A one third of the councillors are elected each year; ☐
  B an election occurs every four years, for all members of the council; ☐
  C another form of election (give details). ☐
_____

9 When are the next elections for your local council?
_____

10 Does your local council have a mayor or a Chair? State which, and give his or her name.
_____

How well do you know Britain's government?

On your own ▸ Choose the correct ending/answer to each of these statements/questions and put a circle round it. Then look up the answers in *Democracy in Action*.

1 The word democracy means …
 a central government   **b** direct government
 c people power
(from page 1)

2 Britain's system of government is a …
 a Presidential system   **b** Constitutional monarchy
 c Dictatorship
(from page 2)

3 The House of Commons is …
 a more powerful than the House of Lords
 b equal in power to the House of Lords
 c less powerful than the House of Lords
(from page 4)

4 The Prime Minister of Great Britain is …
 a the leader of the biggest political party in the House of Commons
 b directly elected by the British electorate.
 c chosen by the reigning monarch

5 In Britain, the Cabinet is made up of …
 a Members of the House of Commons
 b Members of the House of Lords
 c Members of both the House of Commons and the House of Lords

6 How often must there be a General Election?:
 a at least once every four years
 b at least once every five years
 c at least once every seven years
(from page 6)

7 How many MPs are there in the United Kingdom?
 a 651   **b** 659
 c 675
(from page 7)

8 Which system of election is used to elect MPs in a general election?
 a First past the post   **b** The single transferable vote
 c The national list
(from page 9)

9 Which of the following areas does not have a devolved government?
 a Scotland   **b** Wales
 c Cornwall
(from page 11)

10 Which is the largest group of life peers in the House of Lords?
 a Labour   **b** Conservative
 c Independents
(from page 12)

11 What percentage of MPs in the year 2000 were women?
 a 9%   **b** 18%
 c 25%
(from page 14)

12 How many people bothered to vote in the 1997 General Election?
 a 66%   **b** 71.5%
 c 75.5%
(from page 14)

13 What is the biggest way the government raises money?
 a through income tax
 b through VAT
 c through social security contributions
(from page 16)

14 What is the biggest area of government national expenditure?
 a Education
 b the National Health Service
 c Social security
(from page 17)

15 Which political party has been in power for the longest during the last 25 years?
 a The Labour Party   **b** The Conservative Party
 c The Liberal Democrats
(from pages 18–19)

16 Which of the following is not a pressure group?
 a Amnesty International
 b Greenpeace
 c The Scottish National Party
(from pages 20–21)

17 What does a spin-doctor do?
 a manipulate the media
 b run a pressure group
 c run a constituency surgery

18 Which is the biggest tier of local government?
 a District councils
 b Town councils
 c County councils
(from page 24)

19 Which of the following countries is not a member of the European Union?
 a Ireland   **b** Denmark
 c Norway
(from page 26)

20 The Head of the Commonwealth is …
 a The Queen
 b The Prime Minister
 c The Foreign Secretary

Tiebreaker: Name as many members of the British Cabinet as you can.

Citizenship in Focus Teacher's Resources   © HarperCollins*Publishers* 2000

What do you think about the law?

Here are twelve statements expressing opinions about the law.

On your own — Put a tick in one of the columns after each opinion,
saying whether you agree with it, disagree with it or are not sure.

	Agree	Disagree	Not sure
1 The main purpose of the law s to prohibit anti-social behaviour.			
2 Laws should protect you, not restrict you.			
3 You should respect the law, even if you don't agree with it.			
4 Laws on their own won't work. You must have a system of punishment and a means of enforcing it.			
5 Laws are society's way of ensuring justice and that people treat each other fairly.			
6 There are too many laws. If there were fewer laws, society would run more smoothly.			
7 Laws must guarantee individual freedom and, at the same time, protect the vulnerable.			
8 It's your responsibility to obey the law. There can never be any excuse for breaking the law.			
9 Laws shouldn't be altered just because people's attitudes change. If a law is right for one generation, it's right for the next.			
10 Lawbreakers are as entitled to protection by the law as much as law-abiding citizens are.			
11 All countries should have the same laws.			
12 Laws shouldn't tell us how to behave in terms of personal morality, except when our actions affect other people's rights.			

In groups — Take each statement in turn.
Discuss which column you ticked and say why.

29

Time for a change? The child labour laws

CHILD WORKER LAWS TO CHANGE

The British government announced plans yesterday to extend laws covering child employment, two days after a shock survey highlighted poor pay and working conditions for tens of thousands of British children.

Junior health minister Paul Boateng said the government would set working hours and statutory holidays and force councils to draw up lists of jobs that children aged 13 were allowed to do.

They will still be allowed to work 17 hours a week, despite a 1994 European Union directive limiting the hours to 12.

Britain's legislation on working children dates back to the 1930s and allows children aged from 13 to 15 to work outside school hours.

The 1994 EU directive limited the working week for school-age children to 12 hours, but Britain's then Conservative government negotiated an opt-out clause to allow 13-15 year-olds to work up to 17 hours a week with no limits for 15-18 year-olds.

The Labour government's new proposals would set maximum national term-time working hours of two hours per weekday, five hours per Saturday and two hours per Sunday for children aged 13 and over. For children aged 15 and over, the Saturday term-time maximum would be eight hours.

It would also establish maximum national working hours for school holidays of five hours per weekday and Saturday – eight hours per day for over-15s – and two hours for Sundays, with a weekly limit of 25 hours; 35 hours for over-15s.

It would also guarantee children two weeks free from work during school holidays.

The Gulf Today, 14 Feb 1998

In pairs

Study the newspaper article above. Then discuss these questions.

1 The present laws do not allow children to have a part-time job until they are 13. Do you think the law should be changed to allow younger children to work? If so, at what age should they be allowed to work and what sort of jobs would you allow them to do?

2 Make a list of jobs that you think children aged 13 should be allowed to do. What jobs should 13-year-olds be prohibited from doing?

3 What hours do you think children should be allowed to work each week: (a) during term-time; (b) during the school holidays? Do you think children should be guaranteed two weeks free from work in the school holidays?

4 Should there be a minimum wage that employers have to pay schoolchildren, such as £1.50 per hour? Or are there jobs in which it might be appropriate for the employer and the child to agree on a lower rate of pay?

On your own

Draft a statement saying what you think the laws on child employment should be: (a) for children under 13; (b) for children aged 13–15; and (c) for children aged 15 and over. Compare your statements in a class discussion.

Write a letter to your MP saying what you think the laws on child employment should be.

Your rights as a consumer

In pairs

Imagine that you work for a consumer rights magazine. Discuss the letters below, decide what the person's rights are in each case, and draft your replies to them.

Your Letters

Dear Sir/Madam **(A)**

I bought a pair of jeans from the local street market. They were marked inside as being 28" waist and I thought they looked about the right size so I decided to buy them. The stallholder put them in a plain brown paper bag, and I paid cash but he didn't give me a receipt.

When I got home I found they were too tight, so I took them back and asked for my money back or a bigger size. But he didn't have a bigger size and refused to give me a refund. He got quite nasty and even asked me to prove I'd bought them from his stall. What can I do?

Linda Paul
Glasgow

Dear Sir/Madam **(B)**

I bought a pair of good shoes to wear when I go out in the evenings. I wore them once and then noticed that the leather on one shoe seemed to have cracked, so I took them back and complained. The manager said I must have damaged them because they were all right when I left the shop. I demanded a new pair or my money back. I'm sure I didn't damage them and that the leather was faulty. What are my rights?

Steve Collins
Rugby

Dear Sir/Madam **(C)**

I bought a jacket that was reduced in a sale. It was down from £29.99 to £19.99. It fitted me perfectly, but when I showed it to my girlfriend she noticed that the seam down the back was crooked and the material seemed to be fraying. So I went back and asked for a refund, but the manager refused because I'd bought it in a sale. She said I should have realised it was reduced because it was damaged. Am I entitled to a refund?

Winston Charles
London

Dear Sir/Madam **(D)**

I saw a small hairdryer in the window of an electrical shop. It was on special offer so I went in to buy it, but the assistant said it was the last one and he couldn't take it out of the window. He said they'd be getting some more in soon, and they'd be the same price. I told him I'd every right to buy the one in the window and that he was obliged to sell it to me, but he wouldn't. What can I do about it?

Ann Winterton
Derby

Dear Sir/Madam

I recently visited a local high street computer store, with a view to purchasing a game for my video games machine. On trying the game

---

In pairs

Now choose one of these situations and role-play the scene in the shop when the dissatisfied consumer returns to argue with the manager. (This time, of course, the consumer should know what his or her rights are!)

Citizenship in Focus Teacher's Resources

© HarperCollins*Publishers* 2000

Sexual equality and the law

Workplace revolution for women

The government will today support plans for the most radical overhaul of sexual equality laws seen for almost 30 years. The Equal Opportunities Commission is calling for a new equality 'super law' to reflect the dramatic changes in society in the last few decades and to put right the 'outdated' laws which exist.

It will highlight the persisting sexual inequalities in the workplace – such as the 20 per cent pay gap between men and women – and the lack of legislation on harassment.

The commission's proposals to be brought before the Government will include:

☐ A ban on sexual harassment. Currently women have to seek redress through tribunals under the Sex Discrimination Act;

☐ Forcing employers to publish comparisons of pay for men and women and levels of seniority reached by women;

☐ Tightening up rules on clubs and organisations which restrict women membership;

☐ Requirement of all public bodies to promote equal opportunities.

The massive legislative revamp will be the first since the Equal Pay and Sex Discrimination Acts in 1970 and 1975.

The commission will argue that current equal pay legislation is still riddled with loopholes, while tribunal cases against employers – which do not qualify for legal aid – often drag on for years and, ultimately, can only resolve a problem for the employee bringing the case. It will recommend streamlining and simplification of the process, together with a new provision for 'class action'. That would allow employees to bring cases as a group, and mean that the outcome would apply to all those affected.

Guardian, 5 Nov 1998

INSANITY OF SEX BIAS LAW

Businessman Roger Therrien got only half-an-hour's work out of his new assistant – but it cost him £3,500 yesterday.

He became the latest victim of the sex discrimination laws in an extraordinary case that graphically highlights bosses' bitter complaints that they are caught in a Catch-22 situation regarding pregnant employees.

Twenty-year-old Lisa Tomlin successfully sued him after he sacked her 30 minutes into her job when she revealed she was five months pregnant – making her, he says, incapable of carrying out the heavy lifting the job required.

Miss Tomlin had kept her pregnancy a secret at the interview. However, if Mr Therrien had asked her at that time whether she was expecting, then decided not to employ her, he could similarly have been sued for sex discrimination.

Yesterday, after Miss Tomlin was awarded £1,500 by an industrial tribunal, the 52-year-old businessman, who has also paid £2,000 in legal costs, said: 'The law is completely against the employer and that needs to change. I feel like I've been taken for a ride by both the system and this individual.'

Supporters of the law say it stops one of the main forms of discrimination against women, the sacking of pregnant employees.

Equal Opportunities Commission executive Jayne Monkhouse said: 'Somebody doesn't become incapable because they are pregnant. Employers should look towards the long term and have the courage of their convictions when they hire the best person – the great majority of women return to work after maternity leave.'

Daily Mail, 5 Sept 1998

In groups

Study these two articles, then discuss them. Do you agree with the Equal Opportunities Commission's proposals and the reasons behind them? Or do you think the laws on sexual discrimination need to be relaxed rather than strengthened in these ways?

Writing

Write an editorial for a newspaper, **either** (a) commenting on the proposals of the Equal Opportunities Commission, saying how important you think they are and whether or not the government should give them priority; **or** (b) saying what you think of the case of Roger Therrien and Lisa Tomlin.

The law and your personal life

On your own

Here are ten suggestions for changes in the laws relating to your personal life.

Put a tick in one of the columns after each suggestion, saying whether you agree with it, disagree with it or are not sure.

	Agree	Disagree	Not sure
1 You should have to put both the mother's and the father's name on a child's birth certificate.			
2 Adopted children aged 12 and over should have the right to see their original birth certificate and to contact their birth parents, if they wish to do so.			
3 You should be able to get married at 14 with your parents' consent and 16 without their consent.			
4 Before anyone gets married, they should have a blood test and a medical examination.			
5 The legal rights of a couple who choose to cohabit and who have been sharing a place to live for more than six months should be exactly the same as those of a married couple.			
6 When a marriage ends in divorce, any property and assets should automatically be equally divided.			
7 When parents separate or divorce, children aged 13 and over should be able to decide for themselves where they are going to live.			
8 People should be free to make whatever financial arrangements they want with a surrogate mother, and surrogacy contracts should be enforceable in court.			
9 Homosexual couples should be able to marry and, once married, should have the same rights as heterosexual married couples.			
10 Everyone over the age of 18 should have to make a will.			

In groups

Discuss each suggestion in turn.
Explain which of the columns you ticked and why.

How can we reduce crime?

In groups

Study these ten suggestions of ways to reduce crime. Discuss how effective you think each one would be. Can you think of any other measures that would help to reduce crime? Rank the suggestions in order of effectiveness starting with 1 as the most effective. Share your views in a class discussion.

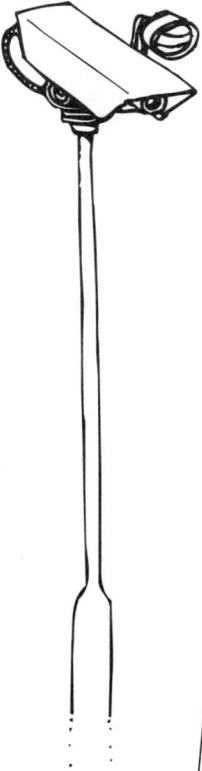

Ten ways to cut down crime

- Increase the size of the police force, so that there can be more police patrols in areas where there is the most crime.

- Give persistent offenders very long sentences if they are convicted of more than three offences.

- Extend Neighbourhood Watch schemes to involve the public more in cutting down crime in their local area.

- Control the behaviour of young offenders by making them observe curfews and tagging them electronically if they don't.

- Reform prison regimes so that prisoners who need it get more psychiatric help and put a greater emphasis on rehabilitating prisoners rather than just locking them up.

- Change the law so that the names of young offenders who commit crimes can be published in the press.

- Offer rewards to members of the public who assist the police in catching criminals.

- Develop the use of new technology, e.g. surveillance and alarm systems to deter criminals and catch more of them on camera.

- Make parents of young offenders more responsible for controlling their children by making them pay fines when their children are convicted.

- Extend schemes that involve criminals meeting their victims and having to compensate them in some way.

Writing

What do you think are the most effective ways of reducing crime?
Write a paragraph expressing your views on how to cut down crime.

The police and you

On your own Here are ten statements about police powers and your rights.

Which ones are true and which ones are false?
Put a tick in the correct box after each statement.

	True	False
1 A police officer cannot stop you and ask for your name and address unless he or she thinks you may have committed a crime.	☐	☐
2 A police officer has the power to search you whenever he or she wants to do so.	☐	☐
3 A police officer cannot force you to go to a police station unless he or she arrests you.	☐	☐
4 If you are being questioned by the police, you have the right to remain silent.	☐	☐
5 The police can take anybody's fingerprints.	☐	☐
6 Young people cannot be interviewed by the police unless an adult is present.	☐	☐
7 The police always need to have a warrant before they can arrest you.	☐	☐
8 If you have committed a minor offence, the police may make a note of it but let you go without pressing charges.	☐	☐
9 Even if you are charged with a serious offence, the police cannot photograph you without your permission.	☐	☐
10 While you are at a police station, you are entitled to free legal advice.	☐	☐

Writing What do you think about the police and their powers? Do the police have too much power or not enough powers? Write a paragraph expressing your views on the police and their powers.

What sentences would you give?

On your own Study the cases (below) and write down what sentence you think the person should receive. Then form groups, compare your ideas and agree on a sentence for each person.

1   Two 19-year-olds break into a factory that has just closed down and do £1000 worth of damage to some machinery. One of them has been cautioned before. It is the other's first offence.

Sentence _____
_____
_____

2   A businessman is convicted of swindling his clients by taking their money and spending it instead of investing it. The sum involved is £40 000.

Sentence _____
_____
_____

3   A 16-year-old takes a sixth-month old car without the owner's consent. He hits a cyclist who is badly injured and crashes the car into a lamppost, causing £3000 of damage. He admits seven other offences.

Sentence _____
_____
_____

4   A young woman who has been in and out of hospital for depression is caught shoplifting in a supermarket. She had put a scarf in her pocket without paying for it.

Sentence _____
_____
_____

5   A 22-year-old man is convicted of being involved in a brawl after a football match, during which he broke an opposing fan's nose.

Sentence _____
_____
_____

6   A teenager admits having bought some ecstasy tablets and having given one to a friend who then collapsed and had to be admitted to hospital.

Sentence _____
_____
_____

7   A man of 25 is convicted of taking part in a robbery, during which he threatened the houseowner with a knife then stole items worth several hundred pounds.

Sentence _____
_____
_____

8   An 18-year-old is found guilty of breaking into a car and stealing a stereo and some tapes. He is a drug addict.

Sentence _____
_____
_____

9   A 23-year-old woman is prosecuted for repeatedly travelling on the bus without a ticket. She is a single mother and she says she couldn't afford the fare.

Sentence _____
_____
_____

10   A man is found guilty of selling goods on a market stall which were proved to be stolen property. Altogether the goods were worth over £1000. He has two previous convictions – one for theft, one for handling stolen goods.

Sentence _____
_____
_____

In the dock: a case study

In pairs

Study the case file of Damien Thompson, a 16-year-old who took a car without the owner's consent. He hit a cyclist, badly injuring her, and crashed the car into a lamppost.

The police charged Damien with dangerous driving, driving without a licence or insurance, taking and driving away a vehicle without the owner's consent, and criminal damage. He was released on bail.

When Damien appeared at the youth court three weeks later he pleaded 'guilty' to all charges.

What sentence would you give him?

Fact file

Name: Damien Thompson

Age: 16 years, 2 months

Address: 64 Fishers Row, Swallowsfield

Education: Swallowsfield High School

Home background: Lives with parents and two older brothers (both unemployed). Mother is a dental receptionist; father recently invalided out of the navy and now living at home

NEWS IN BRIEF

Cyclist injured

A cyclist suffered multiple injuries on Wednesday night when the driver of a stolen car collided with her in Ship Street, Swallowsfield. Nasreen Khaled, 21, of The Green, was taken to Bristol Royal Infirmary, where her condition was later described as serious but stable. The 16-year-old driver of the car, who cannot be named, was charged by the police and later released on bail.

The Swallow

"Damien is generally an attentive student, though his behaviour in recent months has been challenging, and his attendance at school has been patchy. He has cut himself off from his established group of friends and is clearly preoccupied with his home life."

Lisa Evans, Head of Year 11, Swallowsfield High School

"My Audi estate was my pride and joy. One moment it's there, the next it's wrapped around a lamppost, a complete write-off. I can't tell you the amount of time and stress I've spent dealing with all this. Kids like Damien need to be taught a real hard lesson."

Martyn Williams, 39, owner of stolen vehicle

"It was a nightmare. The car just kept coming at me. Luckily it swerved at the last minute, or I would be dead, but I still spent six weeks in hospital and I have a scar on my face that may never disappear. I'd like to sue the boy for damages, but I really don't feel up to it."

Nasreen Khaled, 21, accident victim

Swallowsfield District Council Estimate for repairs	
Repair to lamppost, Ship Street £550	
Repair to railings outside Trinity Rooms, Ship Street	£300
Total	£850

Damien Thompson

Damien has been a model client during the period of probation. He is clearly full of remorse for his actions, and points to severe family difficulties, especially his relationship with his father, causing stress and depression. He has agreed to see a counsellor to explore these difficulties, and his response to them. He has no previous convictions – indeed, no police record of any kind. We would ask the bench to take all of these factors into account when considering this case.

In groups

Role-play the procedure in court from plea to sentence. Apart from Damien (the defendant), you will need three magistrates, a clerk, a prosecuting lawyer and a defence lawyer. Use the information given above, and invent further details where appropriate.

Do different groups pass different sentences? Is this because of the skill of the lawyers, the attitude of the magistrates, or any other factors?

Young offenders – the need for a different approach?

TOUGH SENTENCING WORKS, SAY YOUNG

Young offenders believe that tougher sentences and harsher treatment in detention would deter them from committing a crime, according to a survey.

Up to half of those interviewed said stricter regimes would have a deterrent effect, and some confessed that lenient sentences had actually made them feel easier about offending.

Researchers said some inmates "felt that 'short, sharp, shock' approaches would make some young people realise where they might end up if they continued to offend," said the study, *Wasted Lives*, which is being published tomorrow.

John Greenway, the shadow Home Office minister, said: "This just shows that we have to crack down hard on young offenders. They must be caught and they must know that they will be properly punished. We cannot afford to be soft. We must teach them crime is not acceptable."

Daily Telegraph, 13 Jan 1998

Prisons no place for young offenders, says Prisons Chief

Youth crime is a real problem. Under 17s commit seven million crimes a year, and 26 per cent of young offenders are under 18 years old. But a new report by Sir David Ramsbotham, the Chief Inspector of Prisons, says putting young people behind prison bars does not help. It's much more likely to make them worse.

The idea is to punish them, to protect society from their crimes and to reform them so they won't commit any more crimes. However, seven out of 10 young criminals commit another crime when they leave prison.

Sir David wants a whole new system set up. First he wants children under 18 to be removed from the prison system and held in separate centres not run by Prison Service staff. He also wants the prison service to appoint a Director of Young Prisoners who can see that prisoners under 21 get the treatment they need. The Prison Service is responding by setting up seven or eight juvenile jails, which will hold only those under 18. They want an extra £7000 per year, per teenager, much of which would be spent on improving education and training.

Guardian, 25 Nov 1997

Young thieves made to face their victims

Young offenders will be made to apologise to their victims face-to-face and confront the consequences of their actions in an expansion of a pilot project credited with sharp drops in crime.

Jack Straw, the Home Secretary, will this week sanction the nationwide extension of a scheme designed to steer young people away from a life of crime before they are sucked into the courts process.

He will tell a criminal justice conference that young people who run into trouble with the law should be made to pay back their victim or the community with some form of reparation, possibly involving making good the damage they cause.

The 'restorative justice' project. pioneered by Thames Valley police, has seen the rate of re-offending drop from 35% to 3% and ministers believe it could be a vital tool in nipping crime in the bud.

It involves bringing together young criminals, their parents and all victims who are willing to take part at a meeting in which the consequences of the

Sunday Telegraph, 26 Oct 1997

In groups

Study the newspaper articles above, which describe some of the ways in which young offenders are dealt with by the criminal justice system.

Then discuss the views expressed. Do you have any other suggestions for ways of treating young offenders in order to cut down on the numbers who re-offend?

Citizenship in Focus Teacher's Resources

© HarperCollins*Publishers* 200

The road traffic laws

On your own   Here are ten statements about the road traffic laws. Which ones are true and which ones are false? Put a tick in the correct box after each statement. Then study the information on pages 26–27 of *The Citizen and the Law* and check your answers.

		True	False
1	All vehicles over one year old require an MOT certificate before you can drive them on the road.	☐	☐
2	You can carry a pillion passenger on any size of motorcycle.	☐	☐
3	The Highway Code is part of the law of the land.	☐	☐
4	You must always wear a safety helmet when riding a bicycle, moped or motorcycle.	☐	☐
5	The speed limit on a single carriageway road is 50 mph.	☐	☐
6	If you are convicted of driving without insurance, your licence will be endorsed.	☐	☐
7	You may be liable to disqualification from driving if you get more than 12 points on your licence in a five-year period.	☐	☐
8	You can be arrested if you refuse to take a breath test.	☐	☐
9	If your breath test is positive, the police can ask you for a blood or urine sample.	☐	☐
10	You are not obliged to give your name and address after an accident to anybody except a police officer.	☐	☐

itizenship in Focus Teacher's Resources

You and the law – what should you do if ...?

On your own Here are ten situations. What is the law in each situation?

Write down what you think you should do in each case. Then look up the information on the appropriate page in *The Citizen and the Law* to check whether or not you are right.

1 You have neighbours who keep you awake at night by constantly playing their music very loud. (see page 6)

2 You buy a stereo at a car boot sale and it turns out to have been stolen. (see page 9)

3 You are dismissed from your job without being given any notice. (see page 10)

4 You are constantly the victim of racial abuse from a group of people in the street. (see page 12)

5 You see an advertisement for a job which clearly excludes women from applying. (see page 13)

6 You are on your way home carrying a holdall and a police officer asks you to open it and show them the contents. (see page 18)

7 You are riding a motor cycle which is involved in an accident with a motor car. (see page 27)

8 You want to find out what information about you is held on the police national computer. (see page 30)

9 You discover that someone has put false information about you on their Internet website. (see page 30)

10 You are being taken to court by a neighbour who alleges that you have damaged their fence and you want to know whether you will be entitled to legal aid. (see page 31)

The UN Declaration of Human Rights

Here is an adapted summary of what appears in each article of the United Nations Universal Declaration of Human Rights.

Article 1 – All human beings are born free and equal in dignity and rights.

Article 2 – Everyone is entitled to all the rights outlined in this Declaration, no matter what race, sex, age, religion or colour you are.

Article 3 – Everyone has the right to life, liberty and security of person.

Article 4 – No one shall be held in slavery or servitude.

Article 5 – No one shall be subjected to torture or to cruel, inhumane or degrading treatment or punishment.

Article 6 – Everyone has the right to recognition as a person before the law.

Article 7 – Everyone should be treated in the same way, and laws should apply equally to everyone.

Article 8 – Everyone has the right to legal protection when the law of your country is not respected, and your human rights are ignored.

Article 9 – No one shall be subjected to arbitrary arrest, detention or exile.

Article 10 – Everyone is entitled to a public trial if charged with a crime. This trial should be fair.

Article 11 – Everyone is innocent until it can be proved that they are guilty. Everyone has the right to defend themselves at any public trial.

Article 12 – Everyone is entitled to privacy. No one may enter your house or read your mail without good reasons, or say anything about you that is untrue.

Article 13 – Everyone has the right to freedom of movement and residence within the borders of each state.

Article 14 – Everyone has the right to seek and to enjoy in other countries asylum from persecution.

Article 15 – Everyone has the right to a nationality, that is, to belong to a country.

Article 16 – Men and women of full age, without any limitation due to race, nationality or religion, have the right to marry and found a family.

Article 17 – Everyone has the right to own property, alone as well as in association with others.

Article 18 – Everyone has the right to freedom of thought, conscience and religion.

Article 19 – Everyone has the right to freedom of opinion and expression.

Article 20 – Everyone has the right to freedom of peaceful assembly and association. No one may be compelled to belong to an association.

Article 21 – Everyone has the right to take part in the government of their country, either directly or through freely chosen representatives. Elections shall be held regularly, and everyone's vote is equal.

Article 22 – Everyone has the right to social security, as well as to enjoy cultural activities which help develop their personalities.

Article 23 – Everyone has the right to work, to free choice of employment and to equal pay for equal work. Everyone also has the right to join a trade union.

Article 24 – Everyone has the right to rest and leisure, including reasonable limitation of working hours and periodic holiday with pay.

Article 25 – Everyone has the right to a standard of living adequate for the health and well being of themselves and their family.

Article 26 – Everyone has the right to a free education in primary and secondary school.

Article 27 – Everyone has the right freely to participate in the cultural life of the community, and to share in scientific advances that are made.

Article 28 – Everyone is entitled to a social and international order in which the rights and freedoms set forth in this Declaration can be fully realised.

Article 29 – Everyone has duties to the community. Laws limiting personal freedom shall be restricted to guaranteeing human rights in society.

Article 30 – No one is allowed to destroy, alter or misinterpret any of the rights and freedoms set out in the Universal Declaration.

In groups Which do you think are the five most important articles? When each group has agreed on its list, compare it with the lists of other groups.

The rights of young adults

In groups

Study the following extract from letters written by teenagers from six different countries. Discuss what you learn from them about how the rights of young adults differ from country to country.

Do any of them have rights which you think young people in the UK should have? Are any of them being denied rights which you think they should have?

1 Here in Chicago, we can vote, drive and get married when we're 18. The age of consent is 16. But we're not allowed to drink until we're 21. I think that's good; it prevents drink and drive accidents.

All adults also have the right to carry a gun. You need a gun in America – crime here can be so bad in some of the big cities.

Stacey, USA.

2 All young men over 18 have to do national service in Greece. In other words, you have to be in the army for 18 months. You can start work at 16, but you can't vote until you're 18 and you can't get married without your parent's consent until you're 18.

Nikos, Greece.

3 Here in Saudi Arabia, women of any age must wear clothes that cover our arms and legs in public. Gambling is forbidden and no one is allowed to drink alcohol – it's against Islamic law. I think this is a good thing, because religion is important.

Matima, Saudi Arabia

4 In Calcutta, I think all young people should have the right to a minimum wage. I used to work for less than $1 a day, for eight hours work. Now I'm luckier. But often it's difficult to get work, because I never went to school. I think every child should have the right to an education.

Kishwer, India.

5 In China, you are only allowed one child. This is necessary because we need to keep control of the size of our population. All adults have the right to vote, but the candidates are usually all from the communist party. In politics, you have to support the Communists. This is good, because everyone should take pride in their own political system.

Jan Kim Lee, China.

On your own

Write a letter to someone in another country telling them about the rights a young adult has as a citizen of the United Kingdom, and whether you agree or disagree with these rights.

The right to die

In pairs Look at the following five cases which involve the right to die. Do you think the correct course of action has been followed in each case? Give reasons for your views.

1 A woman and her elderly mother are involved in a serious car accident. Both need immediate medical attention to save their lives. Because the elderly mother is suffering from Alzheimer's disease, the doctor decides to treat the younger woman. Do you think this is the correct decision?

2 *An elderly patient, in a lot of pain, dies from an overdose of painkillers. The doctor who administered the painkillers is charged with murder. At the trial, the doctor is found not guilty because she gave the painkillers primarily to alleviate pain. Do you agree with the court's decision?*

3 A man in a coma dies after his life-support machine is switched off by a local nurse. The nurse claims that the man had requested this in his will, made before he fell into a coma. Although the will has been lost, his wife confirms that this was the case. Do you think the nurse did the correct thing?

4 A young man with a history of mental illness commits suicide, after receiving medical advice from his local doctor on what sort of drugs he should take as painkillers. The doctor confirmed what sort of dose was safe and what was unsafe. The doctor is charged with murder, but found not guilty at the trial due to a lack of evidence. Do you think this doctor should have been taken to court?

5 *A terminally ill patient decides that she wishes her doctor to stop treatment to keep her alive. The doctor, who is deeply religious, refuses, as this is against his religion. The patient requests another doctor who will stop treatment. Do you think the patient should have access to another doctor?*

43

What do you think about freedom of expression?

On your own Study these ten statements about freedom of expression. Put a tick in one of the columns after each opinion, saying whether you agree with it, disagree with it, or are not sure.

	Agree	Disagree	Not sure
1 Young people aged fourteen and above should have completely free access to the Internet.			
2 Press photographers should not be allowed to use zoom lenses to take photographs of famous people on private property.			
3 Anyone should be able to say anything they like about any religion, even if it is blasphemous.			
4 Teachers shouldn't be allowed to discuss homosexuality in schools.			
5 Graffiti should be allowed in some urban areas.			
6 Political protests should be allowed anywhere, provided they are peaceful.			
7 Racists should be banned from speaking in any public building.			
8 The media should be able to publish any story they like, provided it is in the public interest to do so.			
9 When you are twelve, you should be old enough to have a tattoo.			
10 It is unacceptable for men on building sites to whistle at women when they walk past.			

In groups Take each statement in turn. Discuss which column you ticked, and say why.

On your own Choose one statement from the list above with which you either strongly agree or disagree. Write a short summary of why you feel so strongly, giving reasons for your views.

Citizenship in Focus Teacher's Resources

Prisoners of conscience

A prisoner of conscience is a prisoner who is held because of their political, religious or other beliefs, or because of their race, nationality, social status or gender.

Amnesty International, an international human rights pressure group, campaigns to free prisoners of conscience who have not used or encouraged violence. It does this by putting political pressure on any government holding such prisoners. The main method is writing letters.

Letter-writing campaigns target several different groups of people:

1. **The government who is holding the prisoner of conscience.** While some prisoners are not freed immediately, often political pressure leads to better prison conditions.

2. **Other governments,** to increase political pressure for the prisoner to be freed.

3. **Newspapers,** to gain publicity for the prisoner of conscience.

4. **The prisoner,** to keep up their morale and to let them know that something is being done on their behalf.

Dear Sir or Madam,

I am writing to plead for the immediate release of Jon Wang Sun, a local author who has been detained in prison for the last nine months.

As you may know, Jon Wang Sun is a peaceful man, and has no record of ever being engaged in the acts of political violence of which he is charged. As he has been arrested before, and then released without trial, I would urge you to once again examine his case.

Yours faithfully,

Mike Smith
Mike Smith.

A letter to a government holding a prisoner of conscience

On your own Imagine that a military dictatorship is holding a British newspaper reporter, Mel Baker, for reporting on opposition activity in their country. Mel Baker has not broken the law, and has not been charged with any offence. She has now been held for three months.

1 Write a letter to the government who is holding her, asking that she be released. What arguments would you use?

2 Write a letter to your local MP, or a member of the British government. Would you use the same arguments? Would you use stronger language? How would the two letters differ?

3 Finally, write a letter to Mel Baker. What sort of things would you say to her? Remember – your letter may be read by a government official before being given to the prisoner.

45

Capital punishment

In groups Look at the arguments for and against capital punishment (the death penalty). Say which ones you agree or disagree with.

FOR
capital punishment

1 Capital punishment acts as a good deterrent. People are less likely to commit serious crimes if they know that they could be executed as a punishment.

2 The death penalty is right as a matter of justice for murderers. If a person has committed murder, then they too should be killed. 'An eye for an eye, a tooth for a tooth', as it says in the Bible.

3 Keeping murderers and others in prison for life is a drain on our resources, and in some cases crueller than a quick death. What use is a life spent behind bars?

4 In a country with an advanced legal system, the chances of executing an innocent person are absolutely minimal.

5 The death penalty is essential for national security. Without it, there would be no effective way of punishing terrorists, traitors and spies committing treason.

AGAINST
capital punishment

1 Innocent people have died as a result of capital punishment. Far better that convicted criminals are put in jail for life, than an innocent person be murdered by the state.

2 The death penalty is against Article 3 of the UN Declaration of Human Rights, and is not the kind of punishment worthy of a civilised society.

3 There are often numerous appeals against the death sentence. In the USA, a person can be on 'death row', awaiting the results of appeals, for many years. This is mental torture, and a violation of their human rights.

4 The death penalty increases incidences of violent crime. If someone has committed a serious crime, and is on the run, they will resist with more violence if they know the death penalty awaits them if they are captured.

5 The death penalty is not an effective deterrent. Often, those people committing violent crime are under the influence of alcohol or hard drugs. They are not in control of themselves, so they do not think of the legal consequences of their actions.

As a class Hold a debate on the following motion: 'This house believes that capital punishment should be reintroduced into the United Kingdom in the case of mass murder.'

Refugees – what are the facts?

On your own Here are ten statements about refugees. Which ones are true and which ones are false? Put a tick in the correct box after each statement.

	True	False
1 More people leave the United Kingdom each year than arrive in it.		
2 Refugees are a major cause of unemployment in the UK today.		
3 A refugee receives less state benefit than someone from the UK who is unemployed.		
4 Refugees cannot work for the first six months when they arrive in the UK.		
5 Most refugees are simply looking for better work and for more money.		
6 Immigration controls have grown weaker in the UK over the last ten years.		
7 Most refugees are unaware of their legal rights when they arrive in the United Kingdom.		
8 Organised crime is making large profits smuggling immigrants from Eastern to Western Europe.		
9 The number of refugees world-wide has steadily grown over the last ten years.		
10 The United Kingdom has no international responsibilities when dealing with refugees.		

Citizenship in Focus Teacher's Resources

© HarperCollins*Publishers* 2000

Travellers' rights

Travellers told to get off land

A group of travellers is facing legal eviction, with a possible gaol sentence, unless they move off a local estate, it was revealed today.

Three families of travellers have been living for the last five weeks on the edge of an estate in Putteridge, which belongs to the landowner George Graham. The families, who live in a collection of vehicles, include three children, aged 13, 9 and 7, as well as two babies.

George Graham commented: "I've had it up to here with them. Everyone knows the travellers' reputation. They have no right to be living on my land. I have therefore instructed my solicitor to act immediately through the courts. I will be looking to evict them."

Jamie Smith, one of the travellers, said that they would fight any court order forcing them off the land. "It's just fallow field that nobody is using," he argued. "We're doing no harm to anyone. We clean up our own mess. All we want to do is just live our own lifestyle, unmolested – that's all."

George Graham hit back, arguing: "It's my land, and they shouldn't be there. Why should decent ordinary people have to put up with these riff-raff? Would you let people camp on your front lawn?"

Travellers in Karnataka forced to change their way of life

A community of travellers called the Budubudike from the state of Karnataka have had to give up their old way of life. For hundreds of years these travellers moved around from village to village without ever settling in one place. As a member of this community said, 'We used to tell people their fortunes, share stories and play instruments. In return we would be given food and shelter for the night.'

All of this changed, however, when people began to see the travellers as being lazy and living off charity. They were no longer given food or welcomed into people's homes. One of the older travellers said, 'Now we can no longer travel from place to place as we used to.'

The travellers have taken over public land 30 km from Bangalore, the capital city of Karnataka. Most members of their community have taken up farming as a way to make a living. Many of their new neighbours, however, are trying to drive them off this land. They do not want to share land with the travellers because of the way they lived in the past. The travellers believe that they do not have the same rights as everyone else, even after they have been forced to change their way of life.

In pairs

Read the two newspaper articles above.
Then discuss the following questions.

1 Do you think that travellers ought to be able to continue their way of life, or be forced to live on land in one place? Give reasons for your views.

2 Look at the three articles of the Universal Declaration of Human Rights summarised opposite. Do you think that they apply to the rights of the travellers in the two cases outlined above?

> *Article 13* – Everyone has the right to freedom of movement and residence within the borders of each state.
>
> *Article 23* – Everyone has the right to work, to free choice of employment and to equal pay for equal work.
>
> *Article 25* – Everyone has the right to a standard of living adequate for the health and well being of themselves and their family.

48

Racism

1 A British National Party delegate is banned from speaking at a local college. The college officials say this is because he is a racist, and encourages people towards acts of racial violence. Do you agree with the college's decision?

2 A young Chinese woman living and working in Britain complains to an industrial tribunal about jokes that are made about her race. The managing director says that the people in his office were only having a laugh, and that she over-reacted. He claims that there are other Chinese workers who have not complained about these jokes. Do you think that the Chinese worker has a case?

3 A young British student of Afro-Caribbean origin with low grades is awarded a place at a local university. Meanwhile a young student of Asian origin is denied a place even though she has higher grades. The university says it has a policy of positive discrimination towards Afro-Caribbean students, to boost their numbers at this university. Do you agree with the university's actions?

4 A mixed group of teenagers are heading to a football match, shouting and making a lot of noise. Two black police officers decide to stop and question the group. They search two boys, both of them black. When the boys ask why they are being searched, the police officers state that they picked out the two boys because they looked threatening and were creating a disturbance. Do you think the police are acting in a racist manner?

5 A young black woman is cautioned at work for consistently arriving late. Her boss states that 'All black people are late into the office.' The woman argues that she is being picked on, because her boss is stereotyping her. Do you agree with the boss's actions?

In pairs   Above are five cases in which race is an issue. Discuss these cases.

As a class   Now share your views in a class discussion.

How can we improve race relations?

On your own   Look at the following suggestions of ways to improve race relations in Britain. Rank them in order of importance, with the most effective at the top and the least effective at the bottom.

1 Introduce positive discrimination across the British workforce, so that people from ethnic minorities stand a better chance of getting a job.

2 Make it illegal to belong to racist and fascist political groups, such as the British National Party.

3 Recruit more black police officers.

4 Increase the length of gaol sentences for criminals who take part in racist attacks.

5 Introduce a minimum quota to the British parliament, stating that 10% of all MPs must be from ethnic minorities.

6 Spend more money educating and training employers, so that racism in the workplace becomes more detectable.

7 Educate young children about the dangers of racism at primary school.

8 Provide more twinning projects between schools in different communities, so that secondary school pupils can learn more about the traditions, customs and lifestyles of the different ethnic groups in the United Kingdom.

9 Invite former racists who have renounced their views into UK schools, to explain why they now think racism is wrong.

10 Create a minister for equal opportunities, who will oversee the government's efforts to eliminate racism.

11 Have convicted racist criminals walk round town centres wearing a sandwich board, stating their crime, for everyone to see.

12 Make it a criminal offence for any racist material of any description to be distributed on paper, through the media, or on the Internet.

In groups   Compare your views and suggest any other actions that you think could be taken to help to improve race relations in the UK.

50

Facilities for disabled people: a survey

Choose a public building in your area and, using this questionnaire, find out what facilities are available there for people with disabilities.

Name of building: ....

Address: ....

1 How many disabled car parking spaces are there at this building?
A ☐ Two or more
B ☐ One
C ☐ None

2 Look at the entrance to this building. Is there a disabled access ramp for someone in a wheelchair to use?
A ☐ Yes
B ☐ No, but they could manage with a short detour
C ☐ No

3 Are the doors of the building easy to use by someone in a wheelchair or a blind person with a guide dog?
A ☐ Yes
B ☐ They can be used, but with difficulty
C ☐ They cannot be used at all

4 How accessible is the main reception to the building?
A ☐ The reception is on the ground floor, and easily accessible
B ☐ The reception is on another floor, but there is a lift which a disabled person could use
C ☐ The reception is inaccessible for disabled people

5 Look at the main reception desk. Is it easy for someone in a wheelchair to talk to the person at reception?
A ☐ Yes, it would be easy for them to communicate
B ☐ There may be some difficulty in communicating due to the height of the reception desk
C ☐ The person in a wheelchair would not be able to make eye contact with a person sitting at reception

6 Is there someone at reception able to help disabled visitors?
A ☐ There is someone at reception with special information for disabled visitors
B ☐ Someone was able to help, once we had asked, but no special information was available
C ☐ No one was able to help a disabled visitor at reception

7 Is there a hearing loop for deaf visitors?
A ☐ There is a hearing loop in all parts of the building
B ☐ There is a hearing loop in some parts of the building
C ☐ There is no hearing loop in this building

8 How many of the signs inside the building are large and clear for partially sighted or colour-blind people to read?
A ☐ All
B ☐ Some
C ☐ Very few or none

9 How spacious are the rooms and the corridors in this building? Could a person with a guide dog or wheelchair easily use them?
A ☐ Very spacious
B ☐ OK
C ☐ Too cramped and narrow

10 How many disabled toilets are there in the building?
A ☐ At least one, which is easily accessible
B ☐ One, which is fairly accessible
C ☐ None

Mostly As – excellent facilities for disabled people, who would feel welcome at such a building	Mostly Bs – some facilities for disabled people, but several areas need improvement	Mostly Cs – poor facilities for disabled people, who would not feel welcome at such a building

On your own   Look at the answers to your survey. Are they mostly As, Bs or Cs? Use the key above to classify the building.

As a class   Share your results in a class discussion. How impressed are you at the overall level of facilities for people with disabilities in your local area?

Do you know your rights?

On your own Answer these questions by putting a circle round the correct answer. Look in the *Human Rights* book and check your answers.

1 When was the Universal Declaration of Human Rights written?
a 1918   **b** 1945
c 1948   (from page 1)

2 Which of these roles is not part of the job of the UN Commission on Human Rights?
a Monitor countries for human rights abuses
b Lobby to improve human rights across the world
c Intervene in countries to prevent human rights abuses from occurring   (from page 2)

3 Which of the following has never been used to enforce human rights?
a Economic sanctions
b Unarmed observers on the ground
c Nuclear weapons   (from page 3)

4 Which of the following is included in the European Convention on Human Rights?
a The right to own property
b The right to a fair trial
c The right to an education
     (from page 5)

5 How old do you have to be in the UK before you can work?
a 13   **b** 16
c 18   (from page 7)

6 Which of the following rights do children under 16 have in the UK?
a The right to play   **b** The right to leave home
c The right to vote
     (from page 8)

7 Which of the following rights do adults not have in the UK?
a The right to emigrate abroad
b The right to marry
c The right to die   (from page 11)

8 In which country is the death penalty still used?
a The United Kingdom   **b** Switzerland
c The United States
     (from page 13)

9 Which group of people have the lowest minimum wage in Britain?
a Anyone under the age of 18
b Anyone under the age of 25
c Women   (from page 14)

10 What is an asylum seeker?
a Anyone who arrives from another country looking for work in the UK
b Anyone who chooses to move permanently to the UK
c Anyone who applies to stay in the UK for their own protection

11 Which of the following is true about the homeless?
a There are not enough homes to go round in the UK.
b Most homeless people are on drugs.
c There are around 400 000 homeless people in the UK.
     (from page 19)

12 How many children each year die from hunger and poverty related diseases in the world?
a 500 000   **b** 1 million
c 10 million   (from page 20)

13 Which of these rights does a homosexual not have?
a The right to choose their own partners
b The right to work in the armed forces
c The right to adopt children
     (from page 23)

14 How many racist attacks are there in the UK each year?
a 100 000   **b** 210 000
c 330 000   (from page 25)

15 Which of the following is sexual discrimination?
a A woman is paid less than a man per hour, because he has been at the firm longer.
b A woman is sacked from her job because she is caught smoking in a non-smoking area.
c A woman is refused work, because she cannot find someone to look after her children.   (from page 26)

16 Which of the following is true about abortion?
a Abortion is banned in America.
b Both parents have to approve an abortion in the UK.
c There are at least 36 million abortions carried out in the world each year.
     (from page 28)

17 Which of the following rights does a disabled person have in the UK?
a The right to a job
b The right to vote by post
c The right to special seating at public events, e.g. football matches   (from page 31)

18 Which of the following is not a form of torture?
a Being interrogated by police officers
b Placing a black bag over someone's head so he cannot see
c Forcing someone to stand against a wall for hours without a break   (from page 12)

19 Which of the following groups of people have the right to marry in the United Kingdom?
a Homosexuals
b Couples who are separated, but not divorced
c Single parents who already have children
     (from page 23)

20 Which of the following rights is part of the British legal system?
a The right to trial by jury
b The right to remain silent
c The right to a fair and impartial trial
     (from page 13)

Tiebreaker: Name as many human rights included in the Universal Declaration of Human Rights as you can.

Citizenship in Focus Teacher's Resources

The UN Security Council (1)

Background

In 1999, Russia declared war on Muslim rebels in Chechnya, which had tried to declare independence from Russia. During this war, the Russian military fought a long and brutal campaign against the Chechen rebels, who they regarded as terrorists. The Chechen rebels regarded themselves as freedom fighters, who were fighting for their country's independence and the right to control the oil reserves that lie in their country.

In 1999 and 2000, both sides suffered and inflicted heavy casualties. In particular, the civilian population suffered from the Russian air bombardment of the capital Grozny.

The situation

Imagine that this issue is threatening the next round of trade talks at the World Trade Organisation, with European Union states threatening to impose economic sanctions on Russia. Your UN Security Council is set to debate the following resolutions:

a) Russian troops should withdraw from all of Chechnya within two weeks.

b) A UN peacekeeping force, led by NATO countries, should police Chechnya, but allow Russian troops to police Grozny, the capital.

c) Chechen rebels should then hand in their weapons to the UN peacekeepers within a month.

Activity 1

Number of students: 5–12

- Cut up the cards from Copymaster 38 into two piles. Place all of the permanent member cards in one pile, and the non-permanent member cards in another. Deal out the cards, one per person, starting with the permanent member pile first. Do not look at anyone else's card.

- Read the instructions on the card, then role-play a debate within the UN Security Council. You may change or amend any part of the resolution that you wish. You will find the rules for holding a debate on page 19.

- Remember that when it comes to a final vote, any permanent member of the Security Council can veto the resolution, meaning no agreement can be reached. Provided all the permanent members agree, a simple majority of all Council members is then required.

Activity 2

On your own Imagine you were one of the following organisations which had to give evidence on the Chechen conflict to the UN Security Council. Draft a presentation on what you would say, and give reasons for your views.

In groups Now take it in turns to give your presentations on behalf of your organisations. Other students should be allowed to ask questions, to which you should respond.

The United Nations High Commissioner for Refugees, which is concerned at the number of Chechen refugees fleeing the conflict

A Russian Military Commander, who does not want interference in this internal security matter

A Chechen Military Commander, who wishes to protest at the Russian air bombardment of civilians in Grozny

A member of the Muslim charity Red Crescent, which is trying to ensure everyone has safe food and water in the area

The Campaign Against Landmines, which is concerned at the number of landmines being used in the conflict by both sides

A delegate from the Organisation of Arab States, who is worried that some Chechens are being persecuted because of their religion

The United Nations High Commissioner for Children, who is concerned about how children are being affected in the conflict

The United Nations High Commissioner for Human Rights, who is concerned about human rights violations on both sides

The UN Security Council (2)

Russia (permanent member)

You regard Chechnya as a terrorist problem that must be sorted out. With forthcoming Presidential elections, it is important that your government deals sternly with the rebels. You will veto any plan which does not recognise that this is purely an internal Russian security matter.

VETO

China (permanent member)

You have often dealt with internal security problems of your own in the past and so have some sympathy for Russia's position. However, you wish to improve your trading relationship with the United States and the European Union, and so will listen to all sides of the argument.

VETO

USA (permanent member)

You deplore the use of force by the Russians and have forthcoming elections in America. You therefore wish to send American troops as part of a UN peacekeeping force to Chechnya. With the forthcoming trade negotiations occurring, you have an opportunity to influence China, but must not upset the Europeans.

VETO

United Kingdom (permanent member)

You deplore the use of force by the Russians and wish to send a NATO-dominated peacekeeping force to the area. You also wish to increase humanitarian aid to the province and will use your influence with America in the forthcoming trade negotiations to achieve this.

VETO

France (permanent member)

You wish to increase the amount of humanitarian aid in the area and to send UN troops to the area, provided the Americans do not dominate them. You will use the forthcoming trade negotiations with the UK/USA to achieve these goals.

VETO

Mozambique (elected temporary member)

You will listen carefully to everyone's views and support peacekeeping actions, in return for more aid to African countries.

Japan (elected temporary member)

You will usually support America and oppose China. You prefer humanitarian aid to sending UN troops to the region.

Canada (elected temporary member)

As a member of NATO, you will support sending UN troops, provided humanitarian aid is also given.

Ukraine (elected temporary member)

You agree with the Russians that the rebels are a security problem.

Pakistan (elected temporary member)

You think that the Russians should withdraw from Chechnya, and would agree to a UN peacekeeping force which would see many Pakistani troops sent there. You will also agree to spending more money on humanitarian aid.

Egypt (elected temporary member)

You have some support for the Muslim rebels and will agree to humanitarian aid, but are worried about the future role of NATO.

Uruguay (elected temporary member)

You support a quick decision over Chechnya with little money being spent by the UN.

54

Fair trade

What is fair trade?

Fair trade is when the producers of a good, such as farmers in a developing country, receive a fair price for their products. This only happens in a very small minority of cases. Groups such as Third World First and Oxfam are trying to encourage fair trade. One example is Café Direct, a coffee sold in the UK. Similar Fairtrade labelled coffees are sold in 16 other countries. The local farmers in South America receive fair prices for their coffee.

We're going bananas

Bananas are grown in South and Central America, in the Caribbean, and in Africa. Less than one quarter of bananas are eaten in the country where they are grown. The rest are exported abroad. In 1997, over 12 million tonnes of bananas were grown.

Why do developing countries grow bananas?

Often, developing countries are in debt and need to grow crops, such as bananas, which will make money abroad. These crops are known as cash crops. Sometimes the **IMF** or **World Bank** will insist on certain types of crops to be grown, in order for financial aid to be given. As there are a small number of multinationals which control the banana trade, farmers in developing countries have to accept whatever financial terms are offered. They thus receive only a small proportion of the money that the consumer pays.

Guarantees a **better deal** for Third World Producers

Fairtrade

The Fairtrade mark is the independent consumer label that guarantees a better deal for third world producers.

Why is this a problem?

Rather than providing food and sustenance for the local population, farmers concentrate on cash crops for export and are thus vulnerable to exploitation by firms in developed countries.

The problem is further complicated by the size of the banana crop worldwide, which can vary due to the weather. This results in financial instability as the price of bananas goes up and down.

In addition to this, there is a variety of environmental problems that can be caused by the banana industry:

● Waste – for every ton of bananas produced, two tonnes of waste is created. Developing countries do not have the ability to deal with such waste, often contaminated with agricultural chemicals.

● Deforestation – as the demand for bananas rises, so more tropical rainforest is cut down, to create more land for growing.

● Soil contamination – the chemicals used to help grow large bananas can contaminate the soil, making it dangerous for future use.

● Loss of biodiversity – growing bananas across large areas encourages disease and reduces the biodiversity of an area.

What can be done?

In Central and South America, the costs of growing bananas are externalised – the producer does not pay them. Instead, local workers and the local environment suffer. Pressure groups argue that reform needs to occur by internalising costs – forcing banana producers to pay decent wages to local workers and to pay for any damage done to the environment. The latter is known as the 'polluter pays principle'.

(adapted from *New Internationalist*, October 1999, pages 18–19)

In groups

Study the article and then consider what the main problems associated with the banana industry are. What steps do you think need to be taken to ensure fair trade occurs?

Discuss what is meant by the 'polluter pays principle'. Do you think this would be difficult to implement in practice? Why? Give reasons for your views.

As a class

Debate the motion: *This house believes that the government should introduce legislation so that only fair trade products should be sold in our supermarkets.*

Population matters

On your own Look at the following statements and decide which statements are true or false.

	True	False
1 Birth rates are rising in the developing world, and population growth is thus out of control.	☐	☐
2 Over-consumption by developed countries is a greater threat to world poverty than population growth in developing countries.	☐	☐
3 Big families are poorer than small families.	☐	☐
4 The United Kingdom now has a low birth rate and a low death rate.	☐	☐
5 The population of the world is getting older.	☐	☐
6 In the developing world, over one third of the population is under 15.	☐	☐
7 Reducing global population growth could lead to higher resource consumption as lifestyles get better.	☐	☐
8 Every day more children die in developing countries than are born in developed countries.	☐	☐
9 Developing countries cannot cope with massive population growth.	☐	☐
10 The average size of a family is the same across the world.	☐	☐

In groups Discuss what you have learnt about global population trends. Do you think population growth is a real problem? Why? Give reasons for your views.

World hunger

On your own Look at the following statements, each of which would help to reduce world hunger. Rank them in the order that you think would be most effective.

1 Introduce a one-child population policy to all developing countries so that in the long run there are fewer people to feed.

2 Increase research into genetically modified crops so that more food can be grown in less hospitable areas.

3 Encourage intensive farming in famine areas to produce more food where it is needed.

4 Write off developing world debts to discourage farmers from growing cash crops for money.

5 Transfer land from livestock farming and use it instead to grow crops, and encourage those in areas where food is in short supply to become vegetarians.

6 Give away crop surpluses produced within the European Union to developing countries.

7 Provide financial support to developing countries so that they can become self-sufficient in the long run.

8 Double the United Nations peacekeeping budget so that war and regional conflicts do not prevent farmers from growing their crops.

9 Train groups of local farmers to maximise their crop yields by using traditional local growing methods that have worked in the areas previously.

10 Increase the power of the United Nations' World Food Programme so that it can co-ordinate food surpluses to the areas where they are most needed.

In groups Compare your lists and discuss the reasons for your views.

Citizenship in Focus Teacher's Resources

© HarperCollins*Publishers* 2000

Education for all

Learning lies out of reach for 125m of the world's poorest children

Imagine that the entire population of children aged 6 to 14 in Europe and North America did not go to school, but stayed at home or worked. The figure seems incredible, yet that is the fate of an equivalent number of children of primary school age, 125 million, in developing countries.

Imagine also that one in four adults in Britain could neither read nor write, and the number was increasing. But in developing countries, a quarter of adults – 872 million people – are illiterate and there is no sign of anyone producing the funds needed for teachers, books, desks and school buildings, let alone a computer in every class.

Ending this situation would require money, but not – when put into context – all that much. Universal primary education would cost $8bn (£5bn) a year – roughly what the world spends on arms every four days and half what US parents spend on toys for their children annually.

Literacy targets

However, in the developing world, the story is how to get 125 million children – two thirds of them girls – into schools. And what to do about the other 150 million who start school but then drop out.

The people who are denied education will have their human potential destroyed. They will be extremely poor and usually unhealthy. They will die decades earlier than the rest of us. They and their children will be open to exploitation.

Education was recognised as a basic human right 50 years ago in the UN Declaration of Human Rights.

In 1990, the world community promised primary education for all by the turn of the century, to end adult illiteracy. In 1995, that promise slipped by 15 years, to 2015. On present trends, it will slip again.

That is why *The Guardian* backs the Global Action Plan (GAP) proposed by Oxfam and its partners in the developing world. Governments in developed countries would provide an extra $4billion a year through extra aid and debt relief. Developing countries could match that by diverting military spending and other wasteful spending to basic education.

There are vast opportunities for change. In Pakistan, for instance, there are 11 million children out of school. The government spends six times as much on the military as on primary education, and the country has nuclear weapons, which could set off a dangerous arms race in the region.

A commitment to changing attitudes will also have to come from the World Bank and the International Monetary Fund. Both institutions are advocates of transferring financial responsibilities from government to families. This means that many of the world's poorest are asked to pay for their children's education. Many cannot afford to do so, and school enrolment rates have dropped in numerous African countries as a result.

In the twenty-first century, the growth of technology and knowledge-based economies will bring a wealth of opportunities. However, it threatens to exclude great sections of the world's population without the infrastructure of electricity and telephone cables on which it is based. The rest of the world owes them at

(adapted from *The Guardian*, 31 January 2000)

In groups

Read the article and discuss why Oxfam's Global Plan of Action is necessary.

Imagine what it would be like to be unable to read or write, and that you had had no education at all. What difficulties would you face in everyday life? Why?

Imagine you had to give a presentation to a group of children from a developing country who had dropped out of school. What would you say to encourage them to return to school? Why? Give reasons for your views.

Health resources

Euthanasia is a job for executioners not doctors

We hear increasingly of patients being given second rate treatment, or having beneficial treatments withheld, because they are above a certain age.

Prejudice against older people is common in British society, but it influences health care more in some districts that in others. Doctors and other health professionals are trained not to let personal prejudices affect the care they offer to patients. Most of those who institute or condone ageism do so because they think they are performing a public duty to keep down NHS costs.

Ageism is morally wrong because it treats a patient not as an individual but as a member of a group. For an individual patient, benefit from a treatment depends on physiological condition. The risk of physiological impairment increases with age but there is wide individual variation in the rate of ageing.

Using membership of a group to withhold treatment from an individual would cause outrage if grouping was by social class or ethnicity, which are also associated with differences in health care outcomes.

Grosser forms of ageist prejudice are being claimed, including accusations that elderly patients are being killed by starvation orders imposed by nurses. One hopes these will turn out to be based on misunderstandings, but the fact that misunderstandings can arise over such basic issues of patient care indicates a faulty system.

End of life decisions about patients in hospital should be made at consultant level. Consultants should be personally responsible for discussing them with patients and relatives.

Issues surrounding whether treatment is prolonging life or spinning out the misery of a death are particularly worrying matters. These need to be thought out afresh each time they arise. But euthanasia, if it ever comes, will be a job for public executioners, not for doctors.

People aged over 65 comprise more than a quarter of the electorate but British politicians count on older people being too disinterested to vote tactically, as the elderly have done so effectively in America.

By civilised European standards the NHS is underfunded to the tune of 25 per cent or more. While that continues, people who do not make their presence felt politically must expect to be left at the bus stop. Pensioners of the world unite!

(adapted from an article by Sir John Grimley Evans, *The Daily Telegraph*, 7 December 1999)

In groups ▸ Read the article above. Imagine you were in charge of the NHS with limited resources available for operations. Who would you give priority for treatment? Why? Give reasons for your views.

Now imagine you were in the same situation, in a developing country in Africa. Would your decisions be the same? How would they differ? Why?

As a class ▸ Debate the following motion: *This house believes that all healthcare, free at the point of delivery, is a basic human right that everyone should be entitled to, whatever the financial cost.*

A free media?

Project Censored rates the news – again

While the mainstream media and the public focused on President Clinton's sex life, domestic and international events sure to boggle the minds of even the most indifferent went virtually unnoticed by the press last year. We have 'secret negotiations' taking place on the Multilateral Agreement on Investment. There is heedless profiteering from breast cancer by chemical corporations. 'Terminator seeds' are being genetically engineered to control the world's food crops. These were all critical issues left untouched by the mainstream press last year. That is why the media watchdog group Project Censored ranked them as the three most important censored news stories in 1998 in its 23rd annual study,

Censored 1999: The News That Didn't Make the News

In pairs

Read *Project Censored rates the news – again*. Now look at the following newspaper headlines, which were from stories that didn't make the news in 1998. Why do you think such stories were not reported? Who do you think benefits from this? Do you think the public had a right to know in each case? Give reasons for your views.

Secret international trade agreement undermines the sovereignty of nations

Chemical corporations profit off breast cancer

Monsanto's genetically modified seeds threaten world production

Recycled radioactive metals may be in your home

US weapons of mass destruction linked to the deaths of half a million children

Gene transfers linked to dangerous new diseases

United States nuclear programme subverts UN's Comprehensive Test Ban Treaty

On your own

Imagine you were a newspaper editor with the space to report one of these stories on your front page. Which story would you pick? Why? Give reasons for your views.

Using the Cool Planet website

What is Cool Planet?

Cool Planet is a website run by the charity Oxfam. By using the Internet, you can view the Cool Planet website to find out more about the many issues covered in *Global Concerns*.

How do I get there?

Find a computer that has a web-browser open for surfing the Internet. The address for the Cool Planet website is www.oxfam.org.uk/Coolplanet/ Click on Cool Planet for kids.

What should I do when I get there?

If you have been to this website before, have a look at 'What's new?' Websites are being constantly updated, so there's always something new to look at.

Get busy!

Click on 'Get busy'. A whole range of activities is available, for you to try out.

Activity 1: What Oxfam does in different countries

Look at the list of countries that are underlined. Pick a country and click on its name to find out what Oxfam does in that country. Once you have read this information, write a short report to present to the rest of the class.

When the reports are presented, listen to the different work Oxfam does around the world. Is the work Oxfam does in the country you chose the same as in other countries?

Activity 2: What is aid?

Click on 'Understanding aid'. Read the text on understanding what aid is. In groups of three or four, try to answer the multiple-choice questionnaire. Finally, look at the answers and discuss them in your group. Is there anything there that surprised you? Why? Give reasons for your views.

Activity 3: Recycling and fair trade

Work in a group of four and split into two pairs. Pair A should look at 'Recycling' on the 'Get Busy' page, and pair B should look at 'Fair Trade'. Each pair should try to answer the following questions:

a) What is recycling/fair trade?

b) How does it make a difference to the world?

c) Is there anything that we can do to help as individuals?

Use the website links on Cool Planet to visit other sites that deal with these issues. Write a detailed report to present to the class.

Internet issues

Plan to fight child porn criticised

Child protection groups have expressed concern over a controversial strategy being considered by police to fight child pornography on the Internet. It follows reports that British police are considering taking the unprecedented step of posting hundreds of images of abused children on the Net and in other media in an attempt to identify them and prevent further abuse.

But child groups are concerned the strategy could do more harm than good.

'If you can identify them without publishing the pictures, then good. But simply making the pictures public over the Internet or anywhere else is simply a mistake,' John Carr from the charity NCH Action for Children told the BBC's PM programme.

'This is like exposing the children to a double dose of abuse.'

Police from 12 countries, including Britain, are to meet in the new year to decide whether to publish the pictures.

Detective Superintendent John Stewardson of the National Crime Squad said, 'I can see no other way of doing it. I have no background information on these pictures that would lead me anywhere in the world.'

Normally the identities of child sex abuse victims are protected by law. But officers say the parents of the children might be unaware their children are being abused.

The pictures were seized in police raids in 12 countries on the homes of more than 100 suspected paedophiles. The countries involved in the raids included Australia, Austria, Belgium, Britain, Finland, France, Germany, Italy, Norway, Portugal, Sweden and the United States.

BBC, 2 November 1998

Legit hackers roam cyberspace for security

By Paul de Bendern

STOCKHOLM (Reuters) – So you thought hackers were nerds in dark rooms travelling in cyberspace to attack companies' computer systems or steal data. Think again. A new breed of hackers licensed to hack legally into companies around the world, and check their systems' security, is at work in Sweden.

Defcom (www.defcom-sec.com) gets paid for hiring out its 'ethical hackers' to large companies, mostly in the banking, insurance and e-commerce sector around Europe.

'Nine out of 10 companies we're employed to check, we can break into through the Internet,' Defcom chief executive Thomas Gullberg told Reuters. 'That's a frightening statistic.'

Consumers handed an estimated 19 billion pounds over to Internet sites last year, a sign that a lot of people have lost their fears about shopping online. Most got what they ordered and didn't have their credit card details abused.

Licensed to hack

'We've brought hacking to another stage, made it ethical,' Gullberg said. 'We've gathered hackers under one roof. After all they're the best in the business, they know how it's done.'

Defcom's motto, displayed in one of the main hackers' rooms, sums it up: 'It takes one to know one.'

The Swedish company – with an office in London – has grown to over 40 staff, of whom about half are professional hackers, aged 23 to 30. One has a criminal record. The company prefers not to name its hackers, as this may unleash a backlash from real hackers out there seeking to disturb the legitimate ones.

(4 February 2000, Stockholm, Reuters)

In groups

Read *Plan to fight child porn criticised*. Do you think that publishing confiscated material on the Internet will help? Or is this an abuse of the right to privacy? Give reasons for your views.

Read *Legit hackers roam cyberspace for security*. Do you think that it is right for Defcom to employ hackers who have previously committed illegal activities? Or are experienced hackers necessary to provide Internet security? Give reasons for your views.

In pairs

Imagine one of you is a parent and has control over what sites your teenage son/daughter could or could not access on your computer. Make a list of the sites you would ban. Meanwhile, your partner should take on the role of the son/daughter. Make a list of the sites they think they should be allowed reasonable access to.

Compare and discuss your two lists. Are there any differences? Give reasons why you put items on your lists.

Ethical arms

In pairs Look at the following statements. In each case, decide whether you agree, disagree, or are not sure about each statement. Give reasons for your views.

	Agree	Disagree	Not sure
1 Nuclear weapons are a good thing because they prevented war between Russia and America for over 50 years.			
2 The United Kingdom should sell fighter jets to countries like Indonesia and Zimbabwe because if we didn't, another developed country would do so anyway.			
3 We need to continue biological warfare research in order to combat future viruses that may be developed by other countries.			
4 Landmines are a good thing in that they can protect towns by making sure enemy troops cannot cross a particular area.			
5 Chemical weapons are an inhumane way to conduct war and should remain banned in international law.			
6 The UK government should legislate so that companies currently producing arms have to find other goods to produce within the next five years.			
7 The United Kingdom should spend an equal amount on peacekeeping as it does on re-arming itself.			
8 Export licences for UK companies exporting arms to third world countries should be refused, whatever the cost to UK jobs.			
9 UK troops should no longer be allowed to participate in NATO exercises where US troops lay landmines.			
10 All nuclear tests, including tests which don't quite cause a full nuclear explosion (such as the United States has carried out recently), should be banned under international law.			

On your own Pick one or two of the statements above that you feel strongly about. Draft a letter to your MP, explaining why you feel so strongly and what action you feel ought to be taken in this area.

Citizenship in Focus Teacher's Resources

© HarperCollins*Publishers* 2000

What do you know about the world?

1 Which of the following is a developed country likely to have?
   a   A high birth rate   **b**   A high death rate
   c   A high life expectancy
   (from page 1)

2 What do we mean by 'globalisation'?
   a   The rise in interdependence between different governments, corporations and peoples
   b   Environmental events like global warming which affect the whole world
   c   The spread of democracy around the world
   (from page 2)

3 When was the United Nations founded?
   a   1918   **b**   1945
   c   1950
   (from page 4)

4 Which of the following organisations is not part of the United Nations?
   a   The World Food Programme
   b   The World Health Organisation
   c   NATO
   (from page 5)

5 Which of the following countries is a permanent member of the UN Security Council?
   a   Germany   **b**   France
   c   Japan
   (from page 6)

6 What is the Tobin tax?
   a   A tax on environmental pollution
   b   A tax on currency speculation
   c   A tax on corporate take-overs
   (from page 11)

7 Which country will have the largest population in 2025?
   a   Russia   **b**   China
   c   India
   (from page 13)

8 What does 'biodegradable' mean?
   a   A substance free of genetically modified material
   b   A substance that breaks down into harmless chemicals when burnt
   c   A substance that breaks down into toxic chemicals when burnt
   (from page 15)

9 20% of the world's population live in developed countries, but how much of the world's wealth do they own?
   a   20%   **b**   50%
   c   80%
   (from page 17)

10 How much is spent on the global arms trade each year?
   a   £86 billion   **b**   £486 billion
   c   £864 billion
   (from page 24)

11 Which of the following weapons is banned under the 1925 Geneva convention?
   a   Nuclear missiles   **b**   Nerve gas
   c   Hand grenades
   (from page 25)

12 Which of the following activities contribute most to global warming?
   a   Using nuclear energy   **b**   Burning fossil fuels
   c   Cutting down rainforests
   (from page 28)

13 Which of the following countries is the most energy inefficient in the world?
   a   Russia   **b**   USA
   c   China
   (from page 29)

14 What percentage of the world's population will be threatened by rising sea levels during the next 50 years?
   a   10%   **b**   35%
   c   55%
   (from page 28)

15 Which is the biggest criminal problem on the Internet currently?
   a   Credit card fraud   **b**   Pornography
   c   Breach of copyright
   (from page 23)

16 Most of the 30 million people who have HIV world-wide live in …
   a   Africa/South-East Asia   **b**   North America
   c   The former Soviet Union
   (from page 19)

17 People are concerned about GM foods because …
   a   GM foods have been proved to cause cancer
   b   The effects of GM foods are not fully known
   c   Organic farmers may be put out of business
   (from page 15)

18 What is meant by the term 'sustainable development'?
   a   A country that has successfully undergone an industrial revolution
   b   Manufacturing and production that occurs without damaging the environment
   c   The building of new houses on greenfield sites to sustain a country's population
   (from page 30)

19 Which of these acts causes species extinction?
   a   Recycling   **b**   Desertification
   c   Breeding animals in zoos
   (from page 30)

20 What is an interest rate?
   a   The amount of money a bank charges you to borrow money
   b   How much a currency is worth on the foreign markets
   c   The amount prices go up over one year
   (from page 8)

Tiebreaker: Name as many countries as you can that are both members of the European Union and NATO.